# U·X·L newsmakers

10/05

volume **3** three

# McL–Rodd

Judy Galens,
Kelle S. Sisung

Carol Brennan, *Contributing Writer*

Jennifer York Stock, *Project Editor*

**U·X·L**
*An imprint of Thomson Gale,*
*a part of The Thomson Corporation*

REF
920
GAL

**THOMSON**
———★———™
**GALE**

Detroit • New York • San Francisco • San Diego • New Haven, Conn. • Waterville, Maine • London • Munich

## U•X•L Newsmakers

Judy Galens, Kelle S. Sisung, and Carol Brennan

**Project Editor**
Jennifer York Stock

**Editorial**
Michael D. Lesniak, Allison McNeill

**Rights Acquisition and Management**
Peggie Ashlevitz, Edna Hedblad, Sue Rudolph

**Imaging and Multimedia**
Lezlie Light, Mike Logusz, Denay Wilding

**Product Design**
Kate Scheible

**Composition**
Evi Seoud

**Manufacturing**
Rita Wimberly

**LIBRARY OF CONGRESS CATALOGING-IN-PUBLICATION DATA**

Galens, Judy, 1968-

UXL newsmakers / Judy Galens and Kelle S. Sisung ; Allison McNeill, project editor.

  p. cm.

Includes bibliographical references and index.

ISBN 0-7876-9189-5 (set) — ISBN 0-7876-9190-9 (v. 1)—ISBN 0-7876-9191-7 (v. 2)
—ISBN 0-7876-9194-1 (v. 3)—ISBN 0-7876-9195-X (v. 4)

  1. Biography—20th century—Dictionaries, Juvenile. 2. Biography—21st cen-tury—Dictionaries, Juvenile. 3. Celebrities—Biography—Dictionaries, Juvenile. I. Sisung, Kelle S. II. McNeill, Allison. III. Title.

CT120.G26 2004
920'.009'051—dc22

                                    2004009426

Printed in the United States of America
10 9 8 7 6 5 4 3 2 1

# contents

 contents

volume **2** two

volume **3** three

contents

volume **4** four

Italic type *indicates volume number.*

## Art/Design

## Business

## Entertainment

## Government

## Music

## Science

## Social Issues

## Sports

## Writing

**U**·*X*·*L Newsmakers* is the place to turn for information on personalities active on the current scene. Containing one hundred biographies, *U*·*X*·*L Newsmakers* covers contemporary figures who are making headlines in a variety of fields, including entertainment, government, literature, music, pop culture, science, and sports. Subjects include international figures, as well as people of diverse ethnic backgrounds.

## Format

Biographies are arranged alphabetically across four volumes. Each entry opens with the individual's birth date, place of birth, and field of endeavor. Entries provide readers with information on the early life, influences, and career of the individual or group being profiled. Most entries feature one or more photographs of the subject, and all entries provide a list of sources for further reading about the individual or group. Readers may also locate entries by using the Field of Endeavor table of contents listed in the front of each volume, which lists biographees by vocation.

## Features

- A Field of Endeavor table of contents, found at the front of each volume, allows readers to access the biographees by the category for which they are best known. Categories include: Art/Design, Business, Entertainment, Government, Music, Science, Social Issues, Sports, and Writing. When applicable, subjects are listed under more than one category for even greater access.

- Sidebars include information relating to the biographee's career and activities (for example, writings, awards, life milestones), brief biographies of related individuals, and explanations of movements, groups, and more, connected with the person.

- Quotes from and about the biographee offer insight into their lives and personal philosophies.

- More than 180 black-and-white photographs are featured across the volumes.

- Sources for further reading, including books, magazine articles, and Web sites, are provided at the end of each entry.

- A general index, found at the back of each volume, quickly points readers to the people and subjects discussed in *U•X•L Newsmakers*.

## Comments and Suggestions

The individuals chosen for these volumes were drawn from all walks of life and from across a variety of professions. Many names came directly from the headlines of the day, while others were selected with the interests of students in mind. By no means is the list exhaustive. We welcome your suggestions for subjects to be profiled in future volumes of *U•X•L Newsmakers* as well as comments on this work itself. Please write: Editor, *U•X•L Newsmakers,* U•X•L, 27500 Drake Road, Farmington Hills, Michigan 48331-3535; call toll-free: 1-800-877-4253; or send an e-mail via www.gale.com.

U·X·L newsmakers

# Betsy McLaughlin

*c. 1962 • California*

CEO of Hot Topic

**A**s a teenager, Betsy McLaughlin had a plan for her life. She intended to become the chief executive officer (CEO) of a company. She counted on working hard to achieve success, and she expected to make a good living thanks to her hard work. As an adult, McLaughlin has accomplished those goals. Before turning forty, she became the CEO of Hot Topic, a company running a chain of hip, alternative clothing stores for teenagers. She oversaw the tremendous growth of her company, which in 2004 boasted nearly five hundred stores in shopping malls all over the United States. During 2001 McLaughlin led her company's expansion into a new line of stores, called Torrid, which offer plus-size teens the same types of trend-setting fashions sold at Hot Topic. Within two years Hot Topic had opened more than fifty Torrid stores. Named one of *Fortune* magazine's one hundred fastest-growing companies for several years in a row, Hot Topic has succeeded in tapping into the desires of millions of teenagers by energetically seeking out new trends and capitalizing on them before they become too mainstream.

## Betsy's life goals

Elizabeth M. McLaughlin was born around 1962 and grew up in Orange County, California. She was an excellent student, earning straight A's at Estancia High School in Costa Mesa. By the time she graduated from high school in 1978, McLaughlin had mapped out her goals, written on a piece of paper she has carried with her for many years. Among "Betsy's Life Goals," as she termed them, were improving her vocabulary, becoming a CEO by age forty, and learning to be comfortable by herself in social settings. As she told Tiffany Montgomery of the *Orange County Register,* "I knew I'd be working so much I'd need to be OK traveling alone, going to dinner alone."

> **"I don't think we know best. I think we're going to learn so much from [a] customer when that customer walks into our store."**

Her first step in accomplishing her goals was taking a part-time salesperson job at Broadway, a chain of department stores, when she entered college at the University of California at Irvine (UCI). By age twenty, she was an assistant manager at Broadway. After graduating from UCI with a degree in economics, McLaughlin moved up to Broadway's corporate offices, working in the financial and planning departments. She then went to work for Miller's Outpost, a chain of retail specialty stores, and by age twenty-nine she had been named a divisional merchandising manager, making critical decisions about the items being sold in the stores.

In 1993 McLaughlin decided to take a job with Hot Topic, a company she admired. She began as vice president of operations, and spent the next several years working to expand Hot Topic into more and more malls around the United States. In 1992 Hot Topic had fifteen stores; in just over ten years, that number approached five hundred. Her success at Hot Topic led to a series of promotions, with McLaughlin being named president of the company in February of 2000 and CEO just a few months later. Hot Topic appeals to teenagers and young adults who reject a mainstream look and opt for more rebellious, edgy styles, and the culture of the company reflects this unconventional outlook as well. McLaughlin, unlike most executives, does not have a secretary, nor does she have an office. Her desk sits in the middle of a large room, and she works surrounded by the desks of her employees. "Out here," she told Montgomery, "I get the pulse of what's going on."

Founded by Orv Madden in 1989, Hot Topic came about as the result of Madden's conviction that for many teens, clothing preferences are determined by music. Music is still the driving force behind many of Hot Topic's buying decisions. Monitors displaying television music channels like MTV and Fuse can be found throughout Hot Topic's corporate offices. The company will pay for any employee's concert tickets as long as that employee writes up a report about the fashions seen at the show, both onstage and off. McLaughlin explained to Kristin Young of *WWD*, "If [lead singer of No Doubt] Gwen Stefani colors her hair cupcake pink and puts a bindi [a colorful dot often worn by Indian women] on her forehead, we're going to have it first because we were there and saw it first." Hot Topic sells clothing, shoes, and a vast assortment of accessories including jewelry, bags, hats, and posters.

All Hot Topic merchandise is influenced by a variety of alternative music scenes, with about half of the items in the stores—and at the Web site, www.hottopic.com—being licensed merchandise sporting a band's name or logo. Critical to Hot Topic's success has been an ability to spot trends that are on the rise and to quickly have those trends represented in the stores. By featuring merchandise with the logo of a hot new band that has a small but loyal following, Hot Topic stays current and hip. McLaughlin understands that the moment a trend becomes too popular, her core audience will lose interest. Whenever possible, she tries to arrange for exclusive licensing agreements, which specify that for a period of several months, only Hot Topic can sell the official merchandise of a particular band. In addition, she has cultivated relationships with U.S.-based suppliers that result in a much faster turnaround time than that of many other retail stores. It takes anywhere from two to eight weeks from the moment Hot Topic orders a batch of T-shirts or jackets until the time those items appear in stores. For many other kinds of stores, that process can take several months. This speedy ordering time means that Hot

Topic can offer customers the next big thing well before it gets so big that it is no longer seen as cool.

Hot Topic walks a fine line between selling merchandise that appeals to rebellious teenagers and selling items that parents and teachers might strongly object to. The stores do not sell items that encourage drug use or violence, and they avoid merchandise with any kind of religious symbol—aside from those that appear as part of a band logo—in order to prevent the appearance of favoring one religion over another.

## Customers speak

One of Hot Topic's most important avenues of information about what teenagers want comes from the customers themselves. Hot Topic's Web site asks visitors for feedback on a number of issues, from the store's current merchandise to the customer's favorite bands. In the stores, next to the cash registers, customers can find comment cards to mail in to corporate headquarters. McLaughlin spends hours each weekend reading hundreds of comment cards, from which she has gained invaluable information. She told the *Orange County Register,* "The wonderful thing about teenagers is, if you ask, they'll answer. You just have to listen."

One thing many customers requested over and over again was a greater selection of plus-size clothing. With a significant and growing number of teenagers struggling with weight problems, and few stores offering stylish, youthful clothes in larger sizes, Hot Topic recognized a need and leapt to fill it. McLaughlin described to Brent Hopkins of the Los Angeles *Daily News* the limited options available to a young, plus-sized consumer: "She could shop at Lane Bryant and look like her mom, shop at a department store and look like her grandmother, or buy men's clothes and look like her father." Understanding that many teenagers wanted another option, Hot Topic launched a new chain of stores in 2001 called Torrid. Featuring some of the same styles seen at Hot Topic stores, Torrid caters to larger teenagers and young adults, with the typical Hot Topic emphasis on music-influenced trends. The first Torrid store opened in April of 2001 in Orange County's Brea Mall, and dozens of other Torrid stores opened soon thereafter. The new chain was an instant hit with customers. McLaughlin told *People* magazine: "Some people thought we had staged customers because when they went into a store, they saw a mom or daughter screaming with joy or crying." Mary Barker, a Torrid store manager in Northfield, California, explained to Hopkins: "We get an emotional response. We're not just selling clothes, we're really empowering people."

McLaughlin had personally experienced the difficulty of buying clothes in larger sizes, and she felt a deep connection to the development of the Torrid chain, becoming closely involved in its launch. Her attentiveness to her customers' needs has paid off, as have as her flexible business practices and devotion to fostering a creative corporate culture for her employees. The company has shown sales that other retailers can only dream of. Even as mall traffic has slowed, Hot Topic continues to attract ever-larger numbers of shoppers, propelling the company to several years of record growth. McLaughlin occasionally loses sleep worrying about possible pitfalls, such as failing to spot a hip new trend, or confronting a new competitor that swoops in and steals Hot Topic's customers. In an interview with *Wall Street Corporate Reporter,* however, McLaughlin acknowledged the sunny side of her life as Hot Topic CEO: "I am very energized by the chance to lead an organization that gives the customers what they want. Each day of work is filled with high energy and a fast pace. Hot Topic is really a fun place to work."

## For More Information

### Periodicals

Allers, Kimberly L. "Retail's Rebel Yell." *Fortune* (November 10, 2003).

Fosse, Lynn. "Betsy McLaughlin." *Wall Street Corporate Reporter* (November 1, 2000).

Hopkins, Brent. "Hopes High for Torrid Sales." *Los Angeles Daily News* (May 1, 2002).

*People* (May 26, 2003): p. 153.

Young, Kristin. "Hot Topic's New Flame." *WWD* (February 1, 2001): p. 16B.

### Web Sites

Montgomery, Tiffany. "Hot Topic's Latest Venture Finds Big Niche." *Orange County Register.* http://www.ocregister.com/news/torrid00303 cci4.shtml (accessed on July 15, 2004).

Weintraub, Arlene. "Hotter Than a Pair of Vinyl Jeans." *BusinessWeek Online.* http://www.businessweek.com/magazine/content/03_23/b3836 716.htm (accessed on July 20, 2004).

# Mike Mignola

*c. 1962* • *California*

## Comic book author/illustrator

**W**hen first starting out on his career path, Mike Mignola had a modest goal. "All I really want to do is draw monsters," he told Christopher Brayshaw of the *Comics Journal*. Drawn to the comic book industry, one of the few fields where people can create monsters for a living, Mignola figured that, as he told Brayshaw, "maybe after eighty or ninety years I'll have been around long enough that someone will let me do a story." It took far less time than that for Mignola to establish himself as one of the hottest properties in the comics industry, a talented artist who doubles as an intensely creative writer. Mignola's reputation rests largely on his role as the creator of the *Hellboy* series, which features an unusual hero. Sporting red skin, the remains of horns on his forehead, and a tail, Hellboy is a demon—one with very human qualities—who hunts down monsters and other supernatural bad guys. Featured in a number of comic books as well as in several graphic novels, which are book-length comic books that tell an entire story from start to finish, Hellboy also starred in a major motion picture in 2004. Amidst his abundant success, Mignola remains a humble artist who simply wants to spend his life drawing monsters. His efforts just happen to provide extraordinary entertainment for legions of fans.

## Monsters galore

Mignola was born around 1962. He grew up in the Bay Area of California, developing an early passion for monster stories, particularly those in comic books. He experienced a defining moment when, as a sixth grader, he read Bram Stoker's classic horror novel *Dracula*. In an

> "Basically, it's taking everything I've been reading since high school, everything I ever liked, everything I ever read, old movies, tons of pulp magazines and stuff I read in college, fairy tales—all that stuff I've read, going back to *Dracula* in sixth grade, all that stuff I've been thinking about since then, I boiled it all down and made it into *Hellboy.*"

interview with Neda Ulaby on National Public Radio's (NPR) *Morning Edition,* Mignola recalled: "When I read *Dracula,* I said, 'I'm done. I'm done picking that other stuff. I found my thing.'" He explained to Brayshaw, "It's not just that I started liking monsters—it's that I started liking monsters to the exclusion of everything else." His reading choices thereafter consisted of ghost stories and other tales of the scary and supernatural, as well as myths, or ancient stories handed down through the generations, from cultures all over the world.

Mignola knew even during childhood that he wanted to grow up to be a comic book artist. He even knew he wanted to live in New

York City. Growing up in California, Mignola never learned to drive. He explained to Brayshaw that he figured, "'Eventually you're going to live in New York, so don't bother learning how to drive. They have taxis there.'" His lifelong goal—to simply find a job drawing monsters—may seem modest, but Mignola pursued that goal with a passionate intensity. After graduating from the California College of Arts and Crafts in 1982, Mignola headed straight for New York. He had some connections in the comics industry, having done a short inking job for Marvel Comics. His first attempts at finding work were mildly successful, but after six months he returned to California, hoping to obtain long-distance freelance work from the New York-based comics companies. When those offers dwindled, Mignola headed back to the East Coast again, and his persistence finally paid off. He began to get regular work illustrating comic books and covers.

In 1983 Mignola got his first series work as the penciler—the person creating a comic's initial drawings based on the writer's plot—for Marvel's *Rocket Raccoon,* a four-issue work featuring the title character, a time-traveling law enforcement officer. Mignola also worked on several superhero titles and did some illustrating for *The Incredible Hulk* comic books. In 1988 Mignola left Marvel to work for rival DC Comics. At that time, with the 1986 start of Alan Moore's *The Watchmen* and Frank Moore's *The Dark Knight Returns* series, DC had made great strides in the field of comic books and graphic novels aimed at adult readers. The dark, often violent subject matter of such comics appealed to Mignola, and at DC he established his reputation as an exciting and notable artist. He provided illustrations for Jim Starlin's *Cosmic Odyssey* and created the covers for the series *Batman: A Death in the Family.* One of his projects at DC involved plotting a Batman story in which the superhero confronts a ghostly villain. He enjoyed crafting the story's plot as well as creating its images, and began thinking he would like to try it again. A few years later he got that opportunity.

## A demon is born

When film director Francis Ford Coppola began production on the film *Bram Stoker's Dracula* (1992), he called on Mignola to help craft the movie's appearance. Dark Horse, a small, independent comics

## It Takes a Team

Sometimes a comic book or graphic novel reflects the effort of one multitalented person who wrote the story's plot and dialogue and created the illustrations and the lettering. In many cases, however, a comic book is a team effort, with a number of players adding key elements in order to create a vibrant, original work. Each role is dependent upon the other. A glitch at any stage of the process can turn a good story into one that is confusing or sloppy. But when the members of the team work well together, coordinating their creative skills and striving to understand what the others intend to accomplish, the finished product can be magnificent. Below are the primary jobs involved in producing a comic book.

**Writer.** Generally the work begins with the writer, who creates the story, mapping out the details and creating the characters' speech. Often the writer will offer directions about the visual aspects of the story, indicating his or her ideas for how the characters should look or what their movements should be for each panel.

**Penciler.** The illustration work for the comic book begins with the penciler. Just as the writer has used words to tell the story, the penciler must use images. The penciler has a great deal of input on the story's rhythm and pacing, determining, for example, if an action sequence will be spread over just a few panels or over several pages. The penciler also makes decisions concerning the light sources—sunlight streaming through a window, perhaps, or a dark room illuminated by just a desk lamp—and the angle at which the viewer sees the action, whether head-on, from above, and so on. He or she must establish the scene in each panel, carefully choosing which details to draw so that a great deal of information can be communicated without the panel looking overcrowded.

publisher known for creating comic books based on films, signed on for a comic book adaptation of the film, and Mignola was hired to provide the art. With that project, he began a long-running relationship with Dark Horse that would lead to his signature series called *Hellboy.* Mignola had long been toying with the idea of creating a new character. He told Brayshaw, "I wanted to do some kind of monster paranormal investigator," a good-guy creature that would hunt down and get rid of evil creatures. The result was Hellboy, a musclebound demon complete with devilish red skin, horns, and a tail. Raised by decent people, Hellboy thinks of himself as human and is governed by a sense of justice. Part of Mignola's reason for making the main character a monster was to keep up his own interest in drawing the character over and over again; he worried that if he had to draw the same human character repeatedly, he would get bored. In addition, Mignola felt that an otherworldly creature like Hellboy could easily fit into a number of different story lines, and Mignola

**Inker.** After the penciler is finished the work goes to the inker, whose job varies tremendously depending on the style of the penciler. Some pencilers leave a great deal of interpretation up to the inker, while others provide detailed and complete drawings. Generally the inker's job is to finish, polish, or clarify the penciler's work. For example, the inker may take a spherical object drawn freehand by the penciler and use tools to make it perfectly round. The inker provides texture, filling in elements such as hair and fabrics, and depth, which gives readers a sense of each object's position in relation to every other. The inker also adds or elaborates on a drawing's depiction of light and shadow. As suggested by their titles, the penciler creates the image's outlines with pencil, while the inker goes over the existing lines and adds extensive new details in ink.

**Colorist.** Another significant member of the comic book team is the colorist, who, as the name implies, "paints" the images with color. Performing a job that involves far more than simply coloring in, the colorist must study color theory and have an excellent grasp of the depiction of light and shadow. The colorist has a great deal of creative input, making choices that can have a tremendous impact on the book's overall look and mood. While some comic books are still painted by hand, most are colored using a computer. The common use of computers means that colorists, in addition to their painterly skills, must also possess extensive technical knowledge, mastering various software programs and developing techniques for using the technology to its best effect.

**Letterer.** One of the final stages in producing a comic book is the lettering. Lettering involves a number of skills, both artistic and technical. The letterer can act as editor, correcting any mistakes in spelling or grammar. He or she also has input on the font, or the style of the letters, used. The letterer selects the shape of the balloons the words go in, whether it is round, oval, or perhaps square with rounded edges. The letterer also influences the position of the word balloons in each panel, taking care to smoothly guide the reader's eye from one panel to the next.

wanted to incorporate mythologies and folk tales from around the world into the *Hellboy* series. He told Gary Butler of *Rue Morgue,* "From the very start, I wanted to use Hellboy as a device to investigate folklore." Mignola also mixes in healthy helpings of traditional horror stories, particularly those by masters of the genre Edgar Allan Poe (1809–1849) and H. P. Lovecraft (1890–1937), as well as elements from monster comics of decades past.

*Hellboy* initially came about as part of a new imprint, or section, of Dark Horse called Legend. Mignola, along with a group of well-known comic book writers and artists including Frank Miller, Art Adams, and John Byrne, approached Dark Horse with the idea that the new imprint could feature a number of original "creator-owned" series—that is, series that were originated by the writer or artist, rather than new installments of an existing series like Batman. Mignola told Arune Singh of *Comic Book Resources* that his alliance with the more established figures in the comics world made it far easier for him to launch *Hellboy:* "I was the one guy kinda along for the ride, and so you had this high-profile group of people, with the spotlight shining on them because of this Legend imprint, so my book got seen. Without the Legend thing, it might have just been another mini-series from Dark Horse and people saying, 'Oh, there was this demon thing, we don't know what the hell it was.'" When it came to actually writing the first *Hellboy* installment, Mignola felt he needed assistance. He had come up with plots before but had never written an entire comic book. He enlisted the help of Byrne, providing him with detailed notes about plot, design, and even dialogue. While he has acknowledged that Byrne's support and writing help were invaluable, Mignola explained that much of the first book, *Hellboy: The Seeds of Destruction,* came from his own imagination. When it came to writing the second installment, Byrne and Mignola agreed that Mignola would attempt it on his own.

In *Seeds of Destruction,* published in 1994, readers were introduced to Hellboy and given a brief summary of his beginnings. A demon created in hell, the infant Hellboy was summoned to be used as a tool to fight for the Nazis, the ruling party of Germany during World War II, in their quest for world domination. Rescued by American agents from the Bureau of Paranormal Research and Defense, or B.P.R.D., Hellboy was taken back to the United States and raised among humans. In Mignola's universe, the B.P.R.D. is a secret agency that investigates paranormal episodes, or supernatural events that have no logical or scientific explanation. Endowed with a strong sense of duty and fairness, the adult Hellboy combs the globe, investigating these unusual events and hunting down nasty creatures. Hordes of fans were instantly drawn to the *Hellboy* series, attracted not just by the action-packed episodes but by Hellboy's decent, caring nature and mild-mannered, often humorous, approach to life. Mignola told Singh that in some ways Hellboy is based on his father, "who had all these jobs building cabinets and came home busted up, with dry blood all over him, and he was so matter of fact, saying, 'Oh yeah, I got my hand stuck in this machine and all chewed off.'"

Mignola spent the next several years writing and illustrating numerous *Hellboy* issues, gradually revealing details about his demon hero's past. At the beginning of the series, Hellboy refuses to dwell on his evil origins, focusing instead on fighting for good. Over time he is forced to question his true nature, leaving readers to wonder whether he can ultimately escape his fate as a demon created to destroy humanity. Hellboy is aided in his quest by a team of supporting characters, including Abe Sapien, Roger the Homunculus, Johann Krauss, and Liz Sherman.

## Mignola's expanding universe

In addition to commanding a huge audience, Mignola has also earned numerous Harvey Awards and Eisner Awards, prestigious honors in the comics industry. He has continued to write and illustrate *Hellboy* issues, while also occasionally handing over the reins to others. The 2004 issue, *Hellboy Vol. 5: Conqueror Worm,* marked the ten-year anniversary of the *Hellboy* series. Mignola also collaborated with author Christopher Golden on several graphic novels featuring Hellboy, including *Hellboy: The Lost Army* (1997) and *Hellboy: The Bones of Giants* (2001). *Hellboy: Odd Jobs* (1999) is a collection of illustrated short stories written by a variety of authors. With the aid of Golden and several artists, Mignola created a spinoff series focusing on the B.P.R.D. *Mike Mignola's B.P.R.D.: Hollow Earth and Other Stories* (2003) showcased the work of artists such as Ryan Sook and Derek Thompson in a collection of stories highlighting the series' supporting characters.

While *Hellboy* has been the centerpiece of Mignola's professional life, he has also explored other artistic avenues. When work began on Disney's 2001 animated adventure film *Atlantis: The Lost Empire,* the filmmakers initially studied Mignola's work, hoping to imitate his style in the design of the film. Instead they hired the man himself, naming Mignola the film's production designer. His contributions included the design of the characters and input on the film's overall look. The following year Mignola again took a break from *Hellboy* to create *The Amazing Screw-On Head,* a bizarre and amusing story of a mechanical head summoned by President Abraham Lincoln to save the world. An interviewer for *bookmunch* described the work as "one of the finest slices of super-hero surrealism you'll find on your shelves," and labeled it "happily deranged." While *Amazing Screw-On Head* was adored by fans, Mignola refrained from turning the stand-alone comic into a series or adapting it for any other medium, fearful that the magic would be lost. He told Arune Singh,

"There's no plan for more *Amazing Screw-On Head* because I was so happy with what I did with [it] that I'm afraid of spoiling it. I'm very proud of that book."

When the film adaptation of *Hellboy,* directed by Guillermo del Toro, became a reality, Mignola found the notion difficult to believe, because so many earlier plans to film a *Hellboy* movie had fallen through. But the film, based on *Hellboy: Seeds of Destruction,* was finally approved by Revolution Studios and given a hefty $60 million budget. With del Toro as a vocal champion of the film, Mignola had found a dream-come-true partner. The two men clicked from the moment they met, finding that they had surprisingly similar views on how to adapt *Hellboy* to the big screen. Mignola described del Toro to Singh as "probably the only guy out there who loves Hellboy more than I do." From the outset of the project, del Toro insisted on Mignola's close involvement in the film, and requested his approval concerning any departure from the comics version. "The particulars of the story are different," Mignola reported to Murray Whyte of the *Toronto Star,* "but the feel of the thing is the same, and the personality of the character is closer to the personality in the comic than I could have ever dreamed possible."

While fans of the *Hellboy* comics were passionate and fairly numerous before the film was released in the spring of 2004, the film brought the oversized red-skinned hero to the attention of millions, a circumstance Mignola found difficult to grasp. "When I drew the comic, I did it entirely for myself," he told Whyte. "Of course, I hoped people would buy it, but I didn't have commercial potential in mind— if I did, I wouldn't have called it *Hellboy.*" The film's release brought an unusual amount of attention to the comics creator, who told Whyte that following the excitement of the film's premiere he planned to return to his everyday existence and work on new story lines for Hellboy and other characters: "The main difference is I'll now live in a world where people actually know who Hellboy is."

## For More Information

*Periodicals*

Brayshaw, Christopher. "Between Two Worlds: The Mike Mignola Interview." *Comics Journal* (August 1996): p. 65.

"*Hellboy Vol. 5: Conqueror Worm*." *Publishers Weekly* (March 15, 2004): p. 57.

"*Mike Mignola's B.P.R.D.: Hollow Earth and Other Stories*." *Publishers Weekly* (July 21, 2003): p. 176.

Whyte, Murray. "Success Comes to Hero from Hell." *Toronto Star* (April 3, 2004).

### Web Sites

Butler, Gary. "Mike Mignola's Hellboy." *Rue Morgue*. Appears at *Suicide-Girls.com* http://suicidegirls.com/words/Mike+Mignola+on+Hellboy/ (accessed on July 25, 2004).

*Hellboy.com.* http://www.hellboy.com (accessed on July 25, 2004).

"Mike Mignola." *bookmunch*. http://www.bookmunch.co.uk/view.php?id= 772 (accessed on July 21, 2004).

Server, David. "Interview: Mike Mignola." *CountingDown.com*. http:// www.countingdown.com/features?feature_id=2855916 (accessed on July 21, 2004).

Singh, Arune. "A Hell of a Time: Mike Mignola Talks *Hellboy*." *Comic Book Resources*. http://www.comicbookresources.com/news/newsitem. cgi?id=3217 (accessed on July 21, 2004).

Smith, Frank. "Thumbnail: Mike Mignola." *Ninth Art*. http://www.ninthart. com/display.php?article=787 (accessed on July 21, 2004).

### Other

Ulaby, Neda. "Interview: Mike Mignola Discusses *Hellboy* and His Inspiration for Starting the Comic Book." *Morning Edition,* National Public Radio (April 5, 2004).

# Isaac Mizrahi

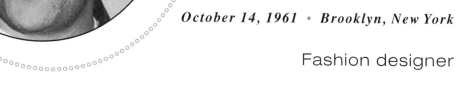

*October 14, 1961* • *Brooklyn, New York*

## Fashion designer

Isaac Mizrahi holds the distinction of being one of today's best-known American fashion designers. His fame comes from far more than his runway creations, however: Mizrahi is a bona fide celebrity who has applied his abundant energy to a number of diverse projects. In 1995, early in his career as a designer, he was the subject of a widely praised film documentary titled *Unzipped.* During 1997 he published a collection of three comic books under the title *Isaac Mizrahi Presents the Adventures of Sandee the Supermodel.* Two years after the 1998 closing of his high-priced clothing design business, Mizrahi explored his love of theater by crafting and starring in a one-man Off-Broadway cabaret show called *Les Mizrahi.* The following year he began hosting his own offbeat talk show, fittingly called *The Isaac Mizrahi Show,* on the cable network Oxygen. During 2004 Mizrahi returned to his fashion-design origins with the launch of two new ventures appealing to very different members of the buying public: an affordable yet fashionable line of clothing for discount retailer Target, and Isaac Mizrahi to Order, a company creating high-end custom-made clothing for consumers willing to spend $20,000 on a single dress. Through all of his various projects, Mizrahi has displayed a fun-loving, humorous, and adventurous style, proving that even high fashion need not take itself too seriously.

## Mizrahi as student

Mizrahi was born in Brooklyn and raised in Ocean Parkway, New Jersey, in a fairly religious Jewish household. He recalled being obsessed with fashion from a very young age, an interest he came by naturally.

> "There is one common philosophy, one thing that you can do no matter who you are or what you look like: You can actually get passionate instead of remaining cool or instead of trying to look like everybody else. You can—you must—immerse yourself passionately in who you are if you want to have style."

His father, Zeke, manufactured children's clothes, and his well-dressed mother, Sarah, often took her youngest child shopping with her in New York's finer shops, including Bergdorf Goodman and Saks Fifth Avenue. In *Unzipped,* Sarah Mizrahi recalled a four-year-old Isaac becoming transfixed by the artificial daisies decorating a pair of her shoes. At the age of eight Mizrahi moved with his family back to Brooklyn. Two years later, after his father bought him a sewing machine, Mizrahi began making clothes for puppets worn during neighborhood birthday parties. By age thirteen he had graduated to making clothes for humans, including himself, his mother, and his mother's friend, Sarah Haddad.

Mizrahi's parents wanted him to get a religious education, and they enrolled him at a nearby yeshiva, a private Jewish school. The somewhat rebellious and flamboyant Mizrahi did not exactly fit in at the conservative school, and he was repeatedly suspended or expelled for impersonating the rabbis and drawing fashion sketches in Bibles. The teachers "thought I was sacrilegious," he told Bridget Foley of *WWD*. "They told my parents I was very abnormal." His parents supported his interest in fashion, but they were determined that he give the yeshiva a chance. Foley explained that "after each of his expulsions, his mother would unzip the high-style creation she had on that day, remove the red nail polish and jewelry, dig up some dowdy dress, and go to the Yeshiva, where she would shake her head and, putting on a pathetic look, make a plea for sympathy." Each time, Mizrahi would be accepted back. Eventually, however, he left the yeshiva to pursue an opportunity much closer to his heart, enrolling at New York's High School for the Performing Arts. There he studied drama, music, and dance, and, after losing seventy-five pounds during his first semester, he developed the confidence to express himself.

Mizrahi soon realized that while he loved the performing arts, his true passion was for fashion design. He began taking evening classes at the highly respected Parsons School of Design. He later studied full-time at Parsons, immediately attracting notice for his sophisticated design skills. After his junior year, Mizrahi landed a part-time job with the esteemed designer Perry Ellis, and worked full-time for Ellis after graduating. Mizrahi worked long hours for Ellis, learning all he could about every aspect of the fashion industry. Though at the time he thought that Ellis asked too much of him, Mizrahi later realized that he owed his mentor, who died in 1986, a great deal. "He was a poet, a real artist," he told Foley. "In retrospect I know I took so much and he gave everything—from exposing me to the fabric market, to teaching me not to be too concerned with what the press expects from you." After leaving Perry Ellis, Mizrahi worked for designers Jeffrey Banks and Calvin Klein.

## Mizrahi as design superstar

In 1987 he started his own business with the financial support of Sarah Haddad Cheney, formerly Sarah Haddad, the family friend who had been a beneficiary of the teenaged Mizrahi's earliest design efforts. He started slowly, crafting his clothes in a rented loft in SoHo, a neighborhood in New York, and delivering his designs from the backseat of Cheney's car. These early designs attracted the notice of many in the industry, and Mizrahi gained the backing of additional investors. He gave his first major show in the spring of 1988, an event attended by only a few members of the press who had taken a chance that something interesting might come from this relatively unknown designer. Those in attendance soon realized that this chance had paid off, as they witnessed the unveiling of a major new talent. His line was widely praised for its fresh approach, combining glamour and elegance with unassuming simplicity. He mixed unusual colors and made use of patterns, including tartan plaid, not generally associated with high fashion. Mizrahi became an overnight sensation, winning the best newcomer award in 1988 and the 1989 award for best women's designer from the Council of Fashion Designers of America (CFDA). He went on to win CFDA's prized Designer of the Year award three times.

Throughout the early 1990s Mizrahi continued to earn praise for his clever, creative designs, while also exploring his love for the performing arts by designing costumes for ballets and other productions. His preparations for the fall line in 1994 were filmed for the documentary movie *Unzipped,* which was released in 1995. Directed by Douglas Keeve, who at the time was romantically involved with Mizrahi, *Unzipped* combined photos and home movies from Mizrahi's childhood with footage of the world-famous designer busily preparing for his upcoming show. In an article written for *Entertainment Weekly,* actress and former model Lauren Hutton declared that *Unzipped* "is the definitive movie about the fashion industry." She went on to report that "it's impossible to resist getting caught up in Isaac's talent and enthusiasm." While some reviewers complained that Mizrahi comes off as annoying and that he and the supermodels who wear his clothes appear whiny and spoiled, others praised the film for its honest look at both the glamour and the competitiveness of the fashion business. The film certainly raised Mizrahi's profile among the general public, transforming him from a successful young designer into a celebrity.

Mizrahi explored other facets of his creativity with the 1997 publication of his book, *Isaac Mizrahi Presents the Adventures of Sandee the Supermodel.* Consisting of three separate comic books packaged together, *Sandee the Supermodel* tells the tale of a beautiful girl from Bountiful, Utah, who is discovered by fashion designer Yvesaac Mizrahi, a character quite similar to the book's author. On her way to becoming a world-famous supermodel, Sandee encounters petty and competitive behavior from her fellow models and struggles with drug problems and an eating disorder. Not long after the book's publication, Mizrahi began working on a film based on the Sandee stories. As his fame spread and fashion editors continued to praise his designs, Mizrahi seemed to have it all. But in 1998 Mizrahi shut down his design business after Chanel, his financial backer, pulled out due to concerns about low sales figures. Upon learning of Chanel's decision to withdraw funding, Mizrahi realized that he had three choices, as he explained to *People* magazine: "One was operating on a shoestring. Another was finding other backers. The third was closing. I thought, 'Move on, darling. Move on.'" And move on he did, choosing as his next adventure a completely new form of self expression.

## Mizrahi as performer

In the fall of 2000 Mizrahi drew on his theatrical education to create a one-man cabaret act, an intimate performance that might be seen in a small nightclub or restaurant. Mizrahi's show, performed in an Off-Broadway theater, combined personal stories with gossip about the fashion industry and classic songs—with lyrics altered to fit Mizrahi's life—from Broadway musicals. Mizrahi also displayed his design skills during the show, drawing quick sketches and using an old-fashioned sewing machine to create articles of clothing. While critics acknowledged that Mizrahi's singing was not his strong suit, many were charmed by his open, engaging, and energetic manner. Such skills came in handy when, the following year, Mizrahi became host of his own television talk show on cable's Oxygen Network. With a steady stream of celebrity guests from the fashion and entertainment worlds, Mizrahi offered audiences an amusing and sometimes odd array of activities. A typical sampling of the shows during the third season featured Mizrahi taking late-night talk show host Conan O'Brien shopping for ties, and teaching *Six Feet Under* star Lauren Ambrose how to knit a hat.

While his television and theater work provided creative satisfaction and, in some respects, offered a welcome relief from the intensity of owning a design business, Mizrahi eventually returned to fashion in 2004 with two very different projects. Bringing high fashion to the average, cost-conscious consumer, Mizrahi launched a line of affordable clothing with a stylish twist, in partnership with Target, the discount retailer. With prices beginning at around $10 and topping out at around $70, Mizrahi's Target line signalled a clear departure from his earlier high-priced designs. For those who wish to spend outrageous sums on clothing, however, Mizrahi began a new service called Isaac Mizrahi to Order. Operating through the upscale department store Bergdorf Goodman, Mizrahi's business offers custom-designed pieces, with prices starting at about $5,000. With a June 2004 show highlighting the Target line as well as newer, high-end items, Mizrahi once again enchanted fashion editors and journalists, reminding observers of what had been lacking during the time when he was absent from the scene. Philip D. Johnson of *Lucire* stated that Mizrahi's return "brought back the keen sense of fun that has been

*Isaac Mizrahi at the launch of his new Isaac Mizrahi Boutiqe for Target.* Dimitrios Kambouris/Wirelmage.com.

sorely missing in fashion in recent years." Both the Target line and the made-to-order service have allowed Mizrahi the freedom to design clothes without having to worry about managing every aspect of a full-fledged design business. The arrangement has freed him up to continually explore new avenues of expression. In the midst of his return to the design industry, for example, Mizrahi prepared to direct his first film, *The Extra Man,* based on a novel by Jonathan Ames.

## For More Information

### Periodicals

Adato, Allison, and Fannie Weinstein. "A Second Act." *People* (August 18, 2003): p. 105.

"Down, Not Out." *People* (October 19, 1998): p. 113.

Foley, Bridget. "Isaac Mizrahi: Setting out for Stardom." *WWD* (April 18, 1988): p. 9.

Hutton, Lauren. "*Unzipped.*" *Entertainment Weekly* (March 8, 1996): p. 73.

"Isaac Mizrahi." *Esquire* (March 2000): p. 192.

Isherwood, Charles. "*Les Mizrahi*." *Variety* (October 30, 2000): p. 34.

Yee, Amy. "Target Hopes to Turn Heads off the Catwalk." *Financial Times* (October 21, 2003): p. 11.

### *Web Sites*

Johnson, Philip D. "The Crown Prince Is Back." *Lucire*. http://www.lucire.com/2003/fall2004/0719fe0.shtml (accessed on July 27, 2004).

# Michael Moore

*April 23, 1954* • *Flint, Michigan*

Filmmaker, author, activist

**R**egardless of whether they agree with his views or not, most people have a strong opinion about Michael Moore. The provocative and controversial social activist has aroused the passionate support of millions, and the equally passionate anger of millions more, with his documentary films, best-selling books, and investigative television shows. Moore has spent his career finding creative ways to address what he sees as the ills of American society: morally irresponsible corporations and a government that responds to small and privileged segments of the population rather than to the needs of the country as a whole. All of Moore's works have sparked controversy and conversation, but his 2004 film *Fahrenheit 9/11* brought a firestorm of heated debate. The film presents Moore's criticism of President George W. Bush, particularly Bush's response to the terrorist attacks in New York City and Washington, D.C., on September 11, 2001, as well as his invasion and subsequent occupation of Iraq in 2003. The controversy over *Fahrenheit 9/11* began with cries of censorship when the Walt Disney Company blocked Miramax, which it owns, from distributing Moore's politically explosive film. As the movie went on to break box office records, the controversy continued, with audiences deeply divided over whether Moore is a creative genius and hero to the average citizen or a manipulative liar and an embarrassment to his country.

## Making a difference

Michael Moore was raised in a working-class family in Davison, a suburb of the economically depressed city of Flint, Michigan. His father worked on the General Motors assembly line for thirty-three

> "I think it would make the founding fathers proud to see the country still survives in their first belief, that's why it's their First Amendment, that somebody has the ability to express themselves and criticize the top guy. That's the country they created."

years, putting together car parts such as spark plugs and oil filters. Moore grew up in a devout Catholic family and attended Catholic primary and middle schools. He was a member of the Boy Scouts and enjoyed such outdoor sports as hunting, even becoming a member of the National Rifle Association (NRA), which he criticized many years later in his film *Bowling for Columbine.* In an interview with Jack Newfield in *Tikkun,* Moore explained that his parents were not especially political, "but they were people who believed in the importance of acting on conscience and standing up for what you believe in." Such principles guided Moore from early on, and while in high school his political activism began to flower. He opposed the Vietnam War (1954–75) and greatly admired the work of the Berrigan brothers, two activist Catholic priests who vigorously protested U.S. involvement in the Southeast Asian conflict. As a teenager

## Documentaries: The New Popcorn Movies

In recent years, the documentary film has enjoyed a surprising rise in popularity. Due in part to the success of films like those of Michael Moore, which are shown in hundreds of theaters all over the country and attract huge numbers of viewers, filmgoers have come to realize that documentaries are not necessarily dry and academic. They can be every bit as entertaining and transporting as a fictional feature film, with certain compelling differences. Documentaries show the lives of real people in real-life situations, with no professional actors and no special effects. In addition, documentaries often have an educational component, bringing to life another time or another place. And documentary films, such as those made by Michael Moore, can bring to viewers a filmmaker's unique point of view. Below is a sampling of documentary films of the early twenty-first century that have attracted critical notice *and* large crowds in theaters.

*Capturing the Friedmans* (directed by Andrew Jarecki, 2003): A disturbing examination of a suburban, middle-class American family torn apart by accusations that the father and one of his sons sexually molested several neighborhood boys.

*Control Room* (directed by Jehane Noujaim, 2004): An in-depth examination of the widely diverging news coverage of the 2003 war in Iraq originating from two sources: the American government and the Middle Eastern network Al-Jazeera, the most popular news source in the Arab world. Noujaim sets out to show that Al-Jazeera, though demonized by the American government as biased and manipulative, strives to present balanced coverage.

*The Corporation* (directed by Jennifer Abbott, Mark Achbar, 2003): An analysis of the far-reaching effects of a U.S. Supreme Court decision that granted corporations the legal rights of an individual, and which shows numerous examples of corporate misdeeds and misinformation.

*The Fog of War: Eleven Lessons from the Life of Robert S. McNamara* (directed by Errol Morris, 2003): An Academy Award–winning reflection, through interviews with the subject and historical footage, on the impact of decisions made by McNamara, the former U.S. Secretary of Defense and one of the architects of the Vietnam War.

*Metallica: Some Kind of Monster* (directed by Joe Berlinger, Bruce Sinofsky, 2004): A film that began as a making-of documentary and turned into a frank examination of the therapy undergone by heavy metal supergroup Metallica. Examines the band's efforts to maintain their integrity as rebellious rockers as they cope with aging and sobriety.

*Spellbound* (directed by Jeffrey Blitz, 2002): An unexpectedly gripping tale of the run-up to the 1999 U.S. National Spelling Bee. Tracks the lives of several young finalists as they prepare for the big contest.

*Super Size Me* (directed by Morgan Spurlock, 2004): A humorous and offbeat film chronicling Spurlock's thirty-day diet consisting exclusively of food from McDonald's. Examines the high rates of obesity in the United States and the role fast-food chains play in such statistics.

Moore believed that entering the priesthood would enable him to make a difference in society just as the Berrigan brothers were attempting to do, and he entered a Catholic seminary to study for the priesthood. He did not complete his study for the priesthood, opting instead to find other ways to effect change.

Upon graduating from high school in 1972, Moore decided to run for a position on the school board in Davison. One of his primary campaign promises was that if elected, he would fire the high school principal. Upset by his tactics, a number of people entered the race hoping to push Moore out of the running. The abundance of candidates served to divide the votes, however, enabling Moore to win the race and become the youngest school board member ever elected in the United States. Moore attended the University of Michigan in Flint for a time, but he did not graduate. He devoted his time to various projects designed to bring to the local citizens a point of view not found in major newspapers or on the television news. He started a weekly alternative newspaper called *Flint Voice* (which later became known as *Michigan Voice*) and established an alternative radio show called *Radio Free Flint*. In 1976 he also opened a crisis intervention center. Moore stayed with the *Flint Voice* as the paper's editor until 1985. He gained exposure on a national level with occasional commentaries on National Public Radio's afternoon news show *All Things Considered*. During 1986 Moore spent four months as an editor at *Mother Jones*, a respected liberal magazine reporting on social issues.

## Entering the national spotlight

After his brief stint at *Mother Jones*, Moore returned to the Flint area. While watching television one day, he saw an announcement from Roger Smith, the chairman and chief executive officer (CEO) of General Motors, or GM, one of the "Big Three" American car companies. Smith announced massive layoffs at a GM plant that would result in many more Flint-area residents joining the ranks of the jobless. The company had closed down Flint plants in favor of opening new plants in Mexico, putting thousands of Michigan residents out of work and devastating the area's economy. Angry about the damage GM's actions had caused in Flint, Moore was determined to do something about it. Knowing absolutely nothing about filmmaking, he nonetheless set out to make a documentary film about the economic problems in Flint, problems that were echoed in many industrial communities all over the country. Moore sought filmmaking help from established documentarians and began raising money to pay for production. He held garage sales, hosted bingo tournaments, and eventually sold his house to help finance the film, which took two and a half years to make and cost $250,000.

*Roger & Me,* released in 1989, caused an immediate stir. Moore has made no claim that his films are objective documentaries; rather, they reflect his strong opinions and personal point of view. With *Roger & Me* and every nonfiction film he has made since, Moore has attempted to provoke audiences to think about and discuss the issues covered, whether they agree with him or not. He has used his sharp wit and assertive personality to showcase what he feels are the evils plaguing society, appealing to viewers' emotions to win support for his causes. In *Roger & Me* Moore spent time with those who had lost their automotive jobs, and examined the bleak economic conditions in Flint following the collapse of much of the area's industry. Moore also sought out a one-on-one interview with Roger Smith, hoping to confront him about the impact the plant closings had had on the community. His inability to secure a meeting with Smith provided many of the film's most humorous moments, and Moore managed to make Smith seem unsympathetic and ridiculous.

Many reviewers praised Moore's debut film, admiring his unique and highly entertaining approach to documentary filmmaking, a genre often accused of being too dry and uninteresting. Many also felt that Moore had examined important social issues and highlighted the price paid by individuals as the result of corporate actions. Others criticized the filmmaker for his obvious bias in favor of average working-class citizens and against corporate executives. Even some who agreed with his politics disapproved of his tendency to make his opponents look foolish on camera, though Moore countered that such people were capable of looking foolish without his help. The *New Yorker*'s Pauline Kael, one of the most significant film critics of the twentieth century, issued a strong condemnation of *Roger & Me,* offended by what she felt was Moore's tendency to talk down even to the out-of-work Flint laborers. Regardless of the debates raging in the media, audiences flocked to the film, which earned more money at the box office than any previous documentary.

## Moore of the same

Moore's next project involved a similar style of crusading for society's underdogs and exposing official wrongdoing. With *TV Nation* Moore tackled numerous subjects over several television episodes aired during the summer of 1994 and again during the summer of 1995. He conducted surprise interviews, staged bizarre stunts with comic results, and generally attempted to make viewers laugh and at the same time feel angry enough about injustices that they might be motivated to act. Several years later, in 1999, Moore returned to television with a comparable program, *The Awful Truth,* which went after such targets as health insurance companies denying patients coverage for critical medical procedures. In the mid-1990s Moore also tackled new types of projects. He directed his first (and so far, only) fictional feature film, *Canadian Bacon* (1995), which starred the late comedic actor John Candy (1950–1994). Moore also wrote his first book, *Downsize This! Random Threats from an Unarmed American* (1996), which described what he saw as inexcusable corporate greed and the mistreatment of American workers. Moore later published other extremely successful books, including *Stupid White Men, and Other Excuses for the State of the Nation* (2002) and *Dude, Where's My Country?* (2003).

While on a book tour promoting *Downsize This!,* Moore shot his next documentary film, *The Big One,* which was released in 1997. *The Big One* covers much of the same territory as *Roger & Me,* with Moore criticizing large corporations for shutting down factories in the United States and moving jobs to countries overseas where labor is far cheaper. The film includes interviews with working-class citizens who lost their jobs due to factory closures or downsizing, which is a term used by businesses to refer to large-scale layoffs intended to reduce that company's workforce. Moore's goal throughout *The Big One* was to interview the CEO of a large company and discuss the impact that the company's actions had on ordinary working citizens. In typical Moore fashion, he pursued such interviews by showing up at CEOs' offices unannounced and trying to argue his way past security guards and secretaries. Phil Knight, the CEO of the athletic goods company Nike, became Moore's primary target, and ultimately Moore was successful in obtaining an interview. He asked Knight about the morality of having all Nike sneakers manufactured outside of the United States. His particular focus was on Indonesian factories, where inadequate or poorly enforced laws allow for child labor and poor working conditions, and where workers earn just a few dollars a day. Knight responded that he felt the factories improved the Indonesian economy and that he felt sure Americans did not want jobs making shoes. Soon after the film's release, Nike changed its policies in Indonesian factories, requiring that employees be at least eighteen years old.

## Taking aim at guns and the president

Moore's fame, and his ability to provoke debate, reached a new level with his documentary film *Bowling for Columbine* (2002). Focusing primarily on the gun culture in the United States, *Bowling for Columbine* examines the issue of gun violence and asks why the rates of gun-related crime are so much higher in the United States than in several other countries where gun ownership is also common. The centerpiece of the film is the 1999 shooting at Columbine High School in Littleton, Colorado. Two students, Dylan Klebold and Eric Harris, entered the school that day armed with guns and explosives, and proceeded to kill twelve students and a teacher before turning their weapons on themselves. In the film, Moore criticizes the wide availability of guns and ammunition, and attacks the NRA for its powerful support of gun ownership and its opposition to any form of gun control.

As with his previous films, *Bowling for Columbine* inspired passionate responses. Many reviewers offered enthusiastic praise for the film, saying that Moore had tackled an important subject cleverly, intelligently, and even at times humorously. Others condemned him for twisting facts through creative editing, leading audiences to reach conclusions that were not necessarily true. For example, the film gives the impression that Charlton Heston, actor and president of the NRA, held a pro-gun rally in Moore's hometown of Flint very soon after a little girl was shot and killed by another child. In fact the rally took place several months after the shooting, and was held in support of the Republican candidate for president, George W. Bush. Many critics and viewers, even those who praised Moore's ability to make a compelling film about important issues, criticized him for his occasionally underhanded tactics, particularly for his tendency to humiliate his opponents on-camera. Many observers also felt that Moore had become a relentless self-promoter, inserting himself into his films whenever possible and taking advantage of every opportunity to get free publicity for his films. Moore has denied that he appears in his films to satisfy his ego. In a 2002 interview with Daniel Fierman of

*Michael Moore poses with his Palme d'Or award for* **Farenheit 9/11** *at the Cannes Film Festival.* AP/Wide World Photos. Reproduced by permission.

*Entertainment Weekly,* Moore, who is a heavyset man known for his somewhat sloppy appearance, asked: "Who thinks that someone who looks like me wants to see himself blown up forty feet on a movie screen? I cringe when I see myself in the movies."

Whether because of the controversy or simply because it addressed a compelling issue, *Bowling for Columbine* drew people to movie theaters in a way few documentary films had ever done before. It won the 2002 Anniversary Prize at the prestigious Cannes Film Festival, where audiences gave the film a fifteen-minute standing ovation after it was screened. *Bowling for Columbine* also won one of the most sought-after awards in the film industry: the 2003 Academy Award for best documentary film. Moore proved himself to be a first class button-pusher when he accepted the award, giving a speech that spoke of his frustration with the disputed results of the 2000 U.S. presidential election. He described President Bush as a "fictitious president" and claimed that the United States had begun the 2003 war with Iraq for "fictitious reasons." While some in the audience cheered his rebellious remarks, others booed. In a 2004 interview with *Entertainment Weekly*'s Fierman, Moore described the general public's reaction to his controversial comments: "For the next couple of months I could not walk down the street without some form of serious abuse. Threats of physical violence, people wanting to fight me.... People pulling over in their cars screaming. People spitting on the sidewalk. I finally stopped going out."

Moore may have felt under attack at the time, but public disapproval did not stop him from undertaking his next hot-button film. In *Fahrenheit 9/11* (2004), Moore's target was none other than the president of the United States. In the film Moore takes issue with President George W. Bush's response to the September 11, 2001, terrorist attacks on the United States. He asserts that the Bush administration took advantage of the American people and offered misleading information to justify the 2003 U.S.-led invasion of Iraq. The controversial nature of the film's subject matter concerned Disney, which is the parent company of Miramax, the studio that financed Moore's film. Disney blocked Miramax from distributing the film, leading to accusations of censorship. Bob and Harvey Weinstein, the heads of Miramax, hastily formed a partnership with other companies to distribute the film, which broke box-office records. In its first weekend it earned more money than any other documentary had made in its entire theatrical run, breaking the record set by Moore's previous film *Bowling for Columbine*. *Fahrenheit 9/11* also won the coveted Palme d'Or, the top prize at the Cannes Film Festival, in 2004.

Once again Moore's detractors insisted that he blew some facts out of proportion and fabricated others altogether, a charge Moore has denied. He told Richard Corliss of *Time* magazine: "There is not a single factual error in the movie. I'm thinking of offering a $10,000 reward for anyone that can find a single fact that's wrong." Moore was also accused of being a traitor and failing to support America's troops serving in the armed services in Iraq. Conservative groups attempted to pressure movie theaters into refusing to screen the film. Moore's fans, on the other hand, cheered his efforts to tell a story that had not been adequately covered by the mainstream news media. Many applauded his message, though not all of his fans appreciated his approach. Some of Moore's supporters have felt that he occasionally goes too far, but Moore remains unapologetic. He does not claim that his films are detached observations of American life; he proudly acknowledges his point of view and owns up to his intention of using film as a medium for change. J. D. Heyman of *People* magazine quoted Moore's comment to ABC news commentator George Stephanopoulos regarding *Fahrenheit 9/11:* "I'm not trying to pretend this is some sort of … fair and balanced work of journalism. I would like to see Mr. Bush removed from the White House."

## For More Information

### Books

*Authors and Artists for Young Adults,* vol. 53. Detroit: Gale Group, 2003.

### Periodicals

Corliss, Richard. "The World According to Michael." *Time* (July 12, 2004): p. 62.

Fierman, Daniel. "Michael Moore." *Entertainment Weekly* (October 25, 2002): p. 43.

Fierman, Daniel. "The Passion of Michael Moore." *Entertainment Weekly* (July 9, 2004): p. 30.

Gates, David, and David Jefferson. "Agent Provocateur." *Newsweek* (June 28, 2004): p. 28.

Heyman, J. D. "Burning Bush." *People* (July 5, 2004): p. 69.

Newfield, Jack. "An Interview with Michael Moore." *Tikkun* (November/ December 1998): p. 25.

### Web Sites

*Internet Movie Database.* http://www.imdb.com (accessed on July 29, 2004).

*MichaelMoore.com.* http://www.michaelmoore.com (accessed on July 29, 2004).

# Frankie Muniz

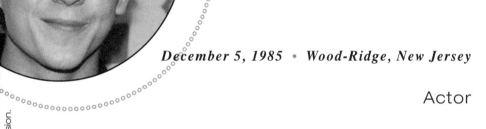

AP/Wide World Photos. Reproduced by permission.

*December 5, 1985* • *Wood-Ridge, New Jersey*

Actor

**F**rankie Muniz initially became famous in 2000 as Malcolm, the boy genius in the Fox comedy *Malcolm in the Middle.* Prior to that role, he had performed in plays, television commercials, and even a few movies. Since the start of *Malcolm in the Middle,* Muniz has spent as much time as possible working, squeezing feature film roles into the months when the television series takes a break. This hectic pace satisfies the teenager, who has energy to burn and claims to hate inactivity. He told Barry Koltnow in a 2002 article for the Knight Ridder/Tribune News Service that he had had only three days off in the year prior, "and I was never so bored in my entire life. I had no idea what to do with myself for those three days." In addition to his role as Malcolm, Muniz has garnered attention for his role as a junior James Bond in two kid-oriented spy movies, *Agent Cody Banks* (2003) and *Agent Cody Banks 2: Destination London* (2004).

## Show-business childhood

Francisco James Muniz IV was born in 1985 in Wood-Ridge, New Jersey. His family—which includes dad Frank, mom Denise, and big sister Christina—moved to North Carolina when Frankie was four years old. A few years later, when he was eight, he watched his sister perform in a local play. He knew immediately that he wanted to perform, and soon after that, he earned his first role, that of Tiny Tim in a regional production of English author Charles Dickens's *A Christmas Carol.* Additional theater work followed, and Muniz began acting in television commercials as well. He started winning parts in films, including the television movies *To Dance with Olivia* and *What the Deaf Man Heard,* both

> **"** I don't consider myself a good actor at all. I just do what I want to do, and I'm just having fun doing it. **"**

broadcast in 1997. At the age of eleven, Muniz moved back to New Jersey with his mother and sister, after his parents had decided to separate. At the same time, he stopped attending school and began to be home-schooled by his mother, an arrangement that gave him the flexibility to accept acting jobs without having to worry about a school schedule.

The acting jobs arrived one right after another, with Muniz appearing as a guest on several sitcoms, including *Spin City.* He began earning more film roles, and appeared in his breakthrough film in 2000. Cast as the young Willie Morris—the author of the autobiographical book the movie was based on—Muniz appeared in *My Dog Skip* alongside Kevin Bacon, Diane Lane, and Luke Wilson. The film, set in the 1940s-era South, depicts the pleasures, fears, and sorrows of Morris's childhood, focusing on the lessons he learned from his beloved dog Skip. While some critics felt the film was a bit sappy and melodramatic, many acknowledged the touching relationship between the boy and his dog. Peter Stack of the *San Francisco Chronicle* praised Muniz's performance: "Frankie Muniz, with vulnerability and wide-eyed innocence, charms as young Willie."

## Muniz as Malcolm

*My Dog Skip* was released during the same year that Muniz began his stint on *Malcolm in the Middle*. When he auditioned for the role, he felt certain he would not get it. Thirteen years old at the time, he thought he was too old to play the much younger Malcolm. The show's producers, on the other hand, knew instinctively that he was the right person for the job. They had prepared themselves for a difficult search to find an actor who could project Malcolm's unusual intelligence and wisdom and yet still be believable as a regular kid with regular kid problems. The show's creator and executive producer, Linwood Boomer, told Brian Raftery of *Entertainment Weekly* that he had asked himself, "Where are we going to find a kid who can do all this?"After seeing Muniz, Boomer knew the search was over: "It was so obvious [it would be Muniz] right from the get-go."

Audiences and critics agreed with Boomer, quickly warming to the young star and appreciating the show's offbeat sense of humor and fresh take on family life. The members of the fictional Wilkersons family included the eldest brother, Francis, who had been sent to military school when the series began; Reese, whose violent tendencies cause many of Malcolm's problems; Malcolm, whose IQ test places him in the genius range and sets him uncomfortably apart from his friends and the rest of his family; and Dewey, who often plays the role of unaffected observer when the family circus reaches catastrophic levels. The constantly squabbling children are led by their father, Hal, who behaves as much like a child as do his children, and their mother, Lois, who rules the household with an iron fist and a raised voice. As Malcolm, Muniz is the voice of reason in an otherwise unhinged family. He often speaks directly to the camera, describing his frustration when things go wrong and his amazement when he gets away with something. Muniz inhabited his character very comfortably right from the start, impressing audiences with his intelligent, wisecracking ways.

## Big-screen adventures

After wetting his feet with *Malcolm* and earning a nomination for an Emmy Award in 2001, Muniz returned to the big screen, starring in *Big Fat Liar* with fellow teen star Amanda Bynes. Muniz plays Jason, a boy from Michigan who enjoys stretching the truth and occasionally

*Frankie Muniz (right) and Antho-*
*ny Anderson in a movie still from*
**Agent Cody Banks 2** *(2004).* ©
MCM Pictures/Corbis.

takes his tales a bit too far. In trouble with his parents and teachers, Jason attempts to fix things by hastily writing a story for school called "Big Fat Liar." Before he has the chance to turn it in, the story is stolen by a once-successful Hollywood producer desperate for a hit. When Jason discovers that his story is the basis for a new movie, he and pal Kaylee (Bynes) take off for Los Angeles, to seek revenge as well as credit for Jason as the story's writer. The film earned many positive reviews, with journalists singling out Muniz for his natural acting and comedic timing. Mick LaSalle of the *San Francisco Chronicle* described the young actor as "spunky and likable, with no weird Hollywood vibe about him."

In his next film, *Deuces Wild* (2002), Muniz plays a young wannabe tough guy caught up in gang conflicts in 1950s-era Brooklyn. The film was not a critical or box office success, but Muniz made up for the disappointment with his next film, *Agent Cody Banks,* released in 2003. Playing the teenaged spy of the film's title, Muniz added to his acting skills with the action-filled role. He spent weeks physically preparing for the role, lifting weights and learning martial arts moves. Muniz plays a character who secretly becomes a CIA agent at the age of thirteen. He has at his disposal a number of nifty gadgets and cool vehicles, but his assignment nonetheless proves difficult, requiring him to excel in his one area of weakness: talking to girls. Banks must befriend an attractive girl, played by teen queen Hilary Duff, to get his hands on her father's invention—which has the power to cause serious global damage if it falls into the hands of the bad guys.

Muniz and the film itself were so successful that the studio, MGM, called for a sequel, with Muniz once again playing Banks. *Agent Cody Banks 2: Destination London* sent the youthful spy across the Atlantic Ocean to once again attempt to save the world from power-hungry villains. Young Agent Banks is paired, to comic effect, with comedian/actor Anthony Anderson, and he once again must navigate conversations with a beautiful girl in the form of British secret agent Emily, played by Hannah Spearritt. The two films combined earned nearly $75 million at the box office, prompting many to speculate on the possibility of a third Cody Banks picture.

Receiving $5 million for the second *Agent Cody Banks,* Muniz is enjoying his wealth and his active lifestyle. He is an avid basketball player and golfer, and has been playing the drums for many years. He has also attracted attention with his passion for cars. Even before he had gotten his driver's license, Muniz had purchased several cars. Among his stable of vehicles is the Volkswagen Jetta driven in the movie *The Fast and the Furious* (2001), which the actor purchased for $100,000, and a rare Porsche that cost the actor $250,000.

Once he turned eighteen, Muniz began thinking more and more about what people had been telling him for years: that he would soon have to make the transition to more adult-oriented fare in order to have a long-term acting career. In a 2004 interview with *Cinema Confidential*'s Shawn Adler, Muniz confessed that he wasn't sure how to proceed or which project to pursue next. "It's tough choosing the right one. It really needs to be something different, but I can't go totally away from my core audience of twelve to eighteen. So it's got to be the right movie that people will look at and not just say, 'Oh, that's him trying to be dramatic. That's him trying to make the transition.' I need to be very believable."

# For More Information

## Periodicals

Bark, Ed. "No Stature of Limitations for *Malcolm* Star Frankie Muniz." Knight Ridder/Tribune News Service (August 13, 2001): p. K4035.

"Brainiacs and Maniacs." *Time* (January 17, 2000): p. 89.

Koltnow, Barry. "*Malcolm in the Middle*'s Star Tries His Hand at Big-Screen Comedy." Knight Ridder/Tribune News Service (February 7, 2002): p. K3059.

LaSalle, Mick. "*Big Fat Liar.*" *San Francisco Chronicle* (February 8, 2002).

Peters, Jennifer L. "Muniz Plays Malcolm." *Know Your World Extra* (February 22, 2002): p. 4.

Raftery, Brian M. "Frankie Goes to Hollywood." *Entertainment Weekly* (January 14, 2000): p. 38.

Stack, Peter. "Uplifting *Skip* Takes a Boy and His Dog into Fresh Territory." *San Francisco Chronicle* (March 3, 2000): p. C1.

## Web Sites

Adler, Shawn. "Interview." *Cinema Confidential.* http://www.cinecon.com/news.php?id=0403092 (accessed on July 27, 2004).

Gallagher, Todd. "10 Burning Questions for Frankie Muniz." *ESPN.com.* http://espn.go.com/page2/s/questions/muniz.html (accessed on July 27, 2004).

# Takashi Murakami

*1962* ∘ *Tokyo, Japan*

Artist

The works of Japanese artist Takashi Murakami have inspired both admiration and confusion. Inspired primarily by *anime,* Japanese animation, and *manga,* Japanese comics, Murakami's paintings and sculptures feature bright, candy-colored images of cartoon-like characters, with large eyes and exaggerated body parts. His works are often decorated with smiling flowers, round, blinking eyes, and colorful mushrooms. Murakami's creations defy traditional classifications, breaking down numerous barriers. He blurs the line between so-called high art—the kinds of works normally seen in museums and galleries—and "low" art, like that seen in cartoons or advertisements. He also contradicts the traditional idea of an artist toiling away in a studio to painstakingly create one-of-a-kind works. Murakami employs a large staff of assistants who help him churn out his designs. Some of his works are extremely high-priced creations intended for a gallery or art collectors, but he also mass-produces merchandise, such as mugs, keychains, and T-shirts, featuring the characters he has created. Murakami is often classified as a pop artist. Pop artists are inspired by popular culture, choosing subjects from such sources as cartoons, billboard advertisements, and consumer goods. He longs for—and in large measure has achieved—a kind of success that few artists realize: he has earned the respect of many in elite art-world circles while also making a good living and becoming hugely popular with the general public.

## A traditional education

Born in Tokyo, Japan, in 1962, Murakami grew up in a household that placed a high value on art. His younger brother, Yuji, also became an

> "I have learned in Europe and America the way of the fine-art scene. Few people come to museums. Much bigger are movie theaters. The museum, that space is kind of old-style media."

artist. Japanese popular culture informed his outlook, but he also felt the impact of Western society, particularly the popular culture of the United States. Murakami became exposed to some aspects of American life during a time when his father worked at an American naval base, and he also absorbed a great deal through imported movies and music. "Only recently did I realize how much I've been influenced by Steven Spielberg," Murakami told *Interview* magazine in 2001. "In his films there is a tension between the children's world and the adults' world." Many of Murakami's works capture that tension between the innocence of childhood and the experience of adulthood, with his cartoon-like images sometimes displaying a dark and slightly creepy undertone.

Murakami wanted to be an artist when he grew up. He was particularly interested in animation and comics, and he felt that studying art would help him improve his drawing skills. He enrolled in the Tokyo National University of Fine Arts and Music in the early 1980s,

## Pop Art

**P**op art, a movement that reached the peak of its influence during the 1960s and 1970s in New York, originated as a rebellion against what some artists saw as a pretentious, elitist art world. Pop artists turned to subjects that had previously been considered unworthy of fine art: consumer products, cartoon characters, and commercial art like that seen on billboards or in magazine advertisements. Pop artists sought to return art to everyday life—or to bring everyday life into the world of art—borrowing images that the general public saw at the grocery store, on the television, or in newspapers.

The person most often associated with pop art is Andy Warhol (1928–1987), an eccentric and ingenious artist who stunned observers with his paintings of Campbell's soup cans and the legendary blonde bombshell Marilyn Monroe (1926–1962). His most famous works involve the repetition of one image with slight variations—the type of soup in *32 Campbell's Soup Cans,* for example, and the colors in *Marilyn Monroe.* He had a crew of assistants that helped create his works at his studio, known as the Factory. Warhol often used photographs as the basis for his paintings and reproduced his works using mass-production techniques rather than working by hand. During his lifetime Warhol was alternately dismissed as merely a commercial artist and embraced as one of the most daring avant-garde rebels of his time. In the years since his death, his tremendous influence on modern art has become widely accepted.

Another successful pop artist was Roy Lichtenstein (1923–1997), best known for his comic-strip-style paintings. Lichtenstein borrowed images from newspaper comics of couples kissing or objects exploding in battle. He used thick, black lines and bright primary colors as well as speech bubbles and sound-effect words like "pow!" to create paintings that divided critics but were hugely popular with the public.

Keith Haring (1958–1990), a successful and somewhat controversial artist in the 1980s, also exemplified the principles of pop art. Using grafitti art as his inspiration, Haring created a collection of familiar images—his radiant baby and barking dog, for example—that he used in numerous works, with slight variations. Like many other pop artists, including Takashi Murakami, Haring caused collisions between high art and low art, creating both museum-quality works and mass-produced merchandise.

Working in a variety of styles and employing a multitude of methods, pop artists have all had one thing in common: the struggle for critical acceptance. Because they refused to accept limited definitions of the types of subjects that are appropriate for works of art, pop artists have been dismissed by some critics as merely illustrators or commercial artists—designations meant to belittle their abilities and demean their work. Over time, however, acceptance of pop art as a legitimate form of fine art has spread, and the pop art movement has, to a large degree, succeeded in bringing popular culture into the realm of high culture.

There he studied *Nihonga,* a nineteenth-century style of Japanese painting that combines Japanese subject matter with European painting techniques. He earned his bachelor of fine arts degree in 1986 and then continued his studies to earn a master's degree in 1988 and a PhD, or doctorate, in 1993. Even while studying *Nihonga,* Murakami began to wonder how meaningful that style was to modern-day Japan. During the early 1990s he continued painting and began to teach drawing, working in the traditional style he had studied at the university while also searching for his own style. Murakami had become increasingly drawn to the world of *manga* and *anime,* and he was also fascinated by the concept of *kawaii,* a Japanese term that translates roughly to "cuteness." Murakami sought ways to incorporate these popular trends into his works to create something of lasting value, as he explained in a 2001 essay, quoted in *Wired* magazine: "I set out to investigate the secret of market survivability—the universality of characters such as Mickey Mouse, Sonic the Hedgehog, Doraemon, Miffy, [and] Hello Kitty."

## Cuteness meets high art

In Japan, the United States, and elsewhere, *kawaii* has proven to be extremely popular, particularly with children and young adults. Japanese characters such as Pokemon and Hello Kitty are used to sell tremendous amounts of merchandise. According to a 2003 article in *U.S. News & World Report,* Hello Kitty appears on some 20,000 products, and annual sales of such products total about $500 million. *Anime* and *manga,* both of which often feature wide-eyed, childlike characters pursuing fantastic adventures, are also connected to the *kawaii* phenomenon. Like Hello Kitty, these cartoons and comics have spawned abundant products—toys, action figures, clothing, and much more—leading to an intensely competitive collecting frenzy. Die-hard collectors not only acquire the merchandise but also accumulate detailed knowledge of the cartoons and comics themselves. This devotion to *anime* and *manga* and to collecting related merchandise is shared by a large community of fans referred to as *otaku.* That term, in combination with "pop," as in pop art, has resulted in a new term, "poku," which could be used to describe Murakami's recognizable artworks.

These works, primarily paintings and sculptures, feature cartoon-like characters painted in bright colors with a shiny, almost plastic-looking surface. Murakami's best-known character is known as Mr. DOB, a mouselike creature with a round head and large, circular ears. Based on a monkey-like cartoon character originally created in Hong Kong, Mr. DOB has appeared in numerous artworks as well as on such

*Commuters look overhead at fiber-glass sculptures by Takashi Murakami on display in Grand Central Station, New York City, in 2001.* © Reuters/Corbis.

merchandise as mousepads, postcards, and T-shirts. Beginning in the mid-1990s, Murakami's works were featured in solo exhibits at galleries and museums throughout Japan as well as in the United States, France, and elsewhere. Some art critics were unsure what to make of these unusual creations: they are highly original, beautifully executed, visually appealing—but can they be considered fine art? Some dismissed Murakami's works, suggesting that they are lovely but lack substance; they please the eye but do not make viewers think. Many others, however, have applauded Murakami's adventurous approach, particularly his ability to bridge the worlds of high and low art and to create works that appeal to a broader audience than most fine art.

Murakami has been particularly praised for his public art—works displayed where they can be seen by all—that inspires a child-like pleasure in viewers of all ages. In the fall of 2003 Murakami installed a public art display called *Reversed Double Helix* at the Rockefeller Center plaza in Midtown Manhattan. The display featured two thirty-three-foot balloons, a number of jewel-colored mushroom sculptures that doubled as seats for visitors, and a twenty-three-foot tall sculpture of Murakami's character Mr. Pointy, known in Japanese as Tongari-kun. Sporting a large round head that comes to a point, multiple arms, and a brightly colored body, Mr. Pointy was described by *People* magazine as "the whimsical love child of Hello Kitty, a Buddha, and a portabello mushroom." Murakami sold the Mr. Pointy sculpture to the owner of the esteemed auction house Christie's for $1.5 million. Two years earlier he had startled and delighted commuters in Vanderbilt Hall, part of New York City's Grand Central Terminal, with *Wink,* a display of mushroom sculptures and huge helium-filled balloons hovering thirty feet off the floor—all of which were decorated with brightly colored eyes of all shapes and sizes as well as spirals and other designs.

## High art meets commerce

While Murakami had become well known in art circles in Japan and the United States by the beginning of the twenty-first century, it was his astonishingly successful handbag designs for Louis Vuitton in 2003 that made him a celebrity—especially in Japan, where he suddenly achieved rock-star-like status. Created in conjunction with designer Marc Jacobs, who was heading up a clothing line for Louis Vuitton, Murakami's designs reinvigorated the stately luxury-goods company, making Louis Vuitton bags the hot new must-have item for the wealthy and fashionable. Murakami applied his trademark use of bright, fresh colors to the traditional intertwined "LV" logo, also incorporating some of his signature images, like wide-open cartoon eyes and smiling blossoms. The first Murakami-designed bags sold out even before they reached stores, and over the next several months the bags—priced in the thousands of dollars—flew off the shelves. Tens of thousands of customers put their names on waiting lists to receive Murakami items from future shipments, and numerous imitation versions sprouted up on big-city street corners and Web sites.

Sales for the Murakami bags made up about ten percent of Louis Vuitton's yearly revenues, totaling well over $300 million in 2003. Murakami paid a price for his success with the Louis Vuitton bags, however: he had achieved widespread fame, but as a designer of purses rather than as an artist. In an interview with Jim Frederick of *Time International* in the spring of 2003, Murakami said: "I need to rebuild the wall between the commercial art and the fine art I do. I need to focus on the fine-art side of me for a while."

Murakami has received almost as much attention for the way his works are produced as for the works themselves. In a style reminiscent of one of pop art's most famous practitioners, Andy Warhol (1928–1987), Murakami calls his studios factories. With one factory located outside of Tokyo and one in Brooklyn, New York, Murakami creates his paintings, sculptures, and merchandise with the help of dozens of assistants. He begins by sketching a design, which he then scans into a computer. He refines the picture on-screen, choosing colors and adding his own trademark images—the mushrooms, happy blossoms, eyeballs, and others—which are selected from a digital file of clip art. The picture is then printed onto paper and handed off to the assistants. They silk-screen the outline onto canvas and begin the laborious process of painting. To achieve the candy-shell high gloss of a Murakami work, the assistants must apply layer after layer of acrylic paint, working with anywhere from seventy to eight hundred different colors for one work. Murakami supervises the assistants' painting but rarely applies it to the canvas himself. He told Frederick of *Time International* that in 1998 he and thirty assistants would spend six months on one large work; five years later, the factories were producing forty works in one year.

Murakami's method of producing paintings results in works that have no depth or perspective—the images seem flat and two-dimensional. Murakami has dubbed this style "superflat," which is, in part, a tribute to the two-dimensional style of some Japanese cartoons. Murakami has also explained the style as a reference to such high-tech devices as flat-screen televisions and computer monitors. The term also reflects the smashing of distinctions between fine art and commercial art, between high culture and low. Murakami told *Interview,* "In Japan, there is no high and there is no low. It's all flat." Jeff Howe wrote in *Wired* that "Murakami likes to flaunt that he can make a million-dollar sculpture and then take the same subject and crank out a bunch of tchotchkes [trinkets]." While his aggressive marketing of his own images and his practice of selling inexpensive knick-knacks alongside his high-priced original works have aroused some controversy in the art world, Murakami sees no reason to change. He told Howe that to him, art is "more about creating goods and selling them than about exhibitions." Undoubtedly he will continue to produce valuable works of fine art as well as inexpensive trinkets, working toward a future where the distinction between the two will be gradually diminished.

## For More Information

### Periodicals

Adato, Allison. "Mr. Pointy." *People* (September 15, 2003): p. 75.

Frederick, Jim. "Move Over, Andy Warhol." *Time International* (May 26, 2003): p. 42.

Howe, Jeff. "The Two Faces of Takashi Murakami." *Wired* (November 2003).

Pagel, David. "Takashi Murakami." *Interview* (March 2001): p. 188.

Rubinstein, Raphael. "In the Realm of the Superflat." *Art in America* (June 2001): p. 110.

Socha, Miles. "The It Bag." *WWD* (December 9, 2003): p. 15.

Terrell, Kenneth. "Art That's Seriously Cute." *U.S. News & World Report* (December 29, 2003): p. 72.

### Web Sites

"Mr. Pointy (and Takashi Murakami) Comes to Rockefeller Center." *The Gothamist.* http://www.gothamist.com/archives/2003/09/08/mr_pointy _and_takashi_murakami_comes_to_rockefeller_center.php (accessed on August 5, 2004).

Wakasa, Mako. "Takashi Murakami." *Journal of Contemporary Art.* http:// www.jca-online.com/murakami.html (accessed on July 29, 2004).

# Walter Dean Myers

*August 12, 1937* • *Martinsburg, West Virginia*

## Author

**W**alter Dean Myers is a pioneer of young adult fiction. His novels about urban teens and the challenges they face have won him both a devoted readership and dozens of book awards. His eighty-plus titles include *Monster, Scorpions,* and a memoir of his own youth, *Bad Boy.* Once thought to have been aimed at the so-called "at-risk" reader, Myers's books have stood the test of time as "poignant, tough stories for and about kids who don't appear in most storybooks," asserted Sue Corbett in a Knight Ridder/Tribune News Service report. "Children whose fathers are absent or jailed. Children who share playgrounds with drug dealers and gangs. Teens struggling to maintain their dignity while living with poverty, violence and fear."

## Raised by another family

Born in 1937, Myers's own early life was marked by challenges, but they were those of a different era. He was born in the midst of the Great

Depression (1929–41), and spent the first few years of his life in a hard-scrabble West Virginia town called Martinsburg. It was about ten miles away from the former plantation on which his ancestors had once toiled as slaves. His family was extremely poor, and his mother died when he was a toddler, while giving birth to another child. A married woman who had been a friend of his mother's, Florence Dean, adopted him. Such informal adoptions were not unusual during the era. Though he was christened Walter Milton Myers, he later substituted "Dean" for his middle name in honor of the foster family who raised him.

> **"I'm not interested in building ideal families in my books. I'm more attracted to reading about poorer people, and I'm more attracted to writing about them as well."**

The Deans soon moved to New York City and settled in Harlem, the northern Manhattan neighborhood that was the center of black life in the city. His foster father, Herbert, worked as a janitor and also in factories, often holding down two jobs to make ends meet. Both he and his wife had little formal schooling, but Florence had taught herself to read, and she then taught her adopted son by letting him read the *True Romance* magazine stories she liked. He progressed to reading comic books, but a teacher discovered him with one in class at P.S. 125 one day. "She grabbed my comic book and tore it up," Myers recalled on a biography that appeared on the Scholastic Web site. "I was really upset, but then she brought in a pile of books from her own library. That was the best thing that ever happened to me." He became a bookworm, and regularly checked books out of his local library—but he carried them home in a paper bag so that other kids would not tease him.

## A caring community

Although Harlem would later become a violent, drug-troubled area, it was a far more balanced community when Myers was growing up

## Major Works by Myers

*Fast Sam, Cool Clyde, and Stuff* (novel), Viking Press, 1975.

*Mojo and the Russians* (novel), Viking Press, 1977.

*Hoops* (novel), Delacorte Press, 1981.

*Fallen Angels* (novel), Scholastic, 1988.

*The Great Migration: An American Story* (poems; paintings by Jacob Lawrence), HarperCollins, 1993.

*Malcolm X: By Any Means Necessary* (biography), Scholastic, 1993.

*The Glory Field* (novel), Scholastic, 1994.

*Slam!* (novel), Scholastic, 1996.

*Harlem: A Poem,* illustrated by Christopher Myers, Scholastic, 1997.

*Amistad: A Long Road to Freedom* (nonfiction), Dutton, 1998.

*At Her Majesty's Request: An African Princess in Victorian England* (nonfiction), Scholastic, 1999.

*Monster* (novel; illustrated by Christopher Myers), HarperCollins, 1999.

*145th Street: Short Stories,* Delacorte Press, 2000.

*The Blues of Flats Brown* (picture book; illustrated by Nina Laden), Holiday House, 2000.

*Bad Boy: A Memoir,* HarperCollins, 2001.

*Handbook for Boys* (novel), HarperCollins, 2002.

there. Because neighborhoods elsewhere were not welcoming to African Americans, Harlem was home to black judges, doctors, and other professionals, as well as to ordinary working families. Myers even lived near the poet Langston Hughes (1902–1967). Hughes was one of the leading names of the Harlem Renaissance, the flourishing of African American music, literature, and other forms of art that began in the 1920s. Myers once spied the famous writer sitting on his front steps "drinking beer, but I didn't think much of him," he told Jennifer M. Brown in a *Publishers Weekly* interview. "He didn't fit my stereotype of what serious writers should be. He wasn't writing about Venice."

Myers retreated into books in part because he suffered from a speech impediment. When other kids made fun of him, he sometimes hit them. One teacher realized he could read aloud in class with little difficulty if he was reading words that he had written himself, and encouraged him to write more. Another teacher found a speech therapist for Myers, and also channeled the child's bossy nature into a role as the class leader. "He gave me permission to be a bright kid, permission to be smart," a *Milwaukee Journal Sentinel* article by Jim Higgins quoted Myers as saying.

During his teens Myers became disillusioned over his lot in life. He continued to get into trouble at school, and realized that not many avenues would be open to him once he left high school. Even though he was a bright student, he knew there were few resources available for blacks. "My folks couldn't send me to even a free college," he told Amanda Smith in *Publishers Weekly.* "There were days when I didn't have clothing to wear to high school, and I just didn't go." He dropped out of Stuyvesant High School, and, on his seventeenth birthday in 1954, he enlisted in the Army. He served three years and returned to New York City to take a series of low-paying jobs. He worked in the post office, as a messenger, and as a factory interviewer for the New York State Bureau of Labor.

## Entered writing contest

Myers had been writing since his school days, and had even won awards for his work. He had never thought that his short stories could provide a career for him, but in the 1960s he began to submit his work to magazines. He also found freelance work for publications like the *National Enquirer.* In 1968 he entered and won a competition sponsored by the Council on Interracial Books for Children for African-American writers. His winning entry became a picture book, *Where Does the Day Go?* Its simple, charming plot involves a walk in the park led by a kindly African American dad; he takes along several children from different ethnic backgrounds, and all offer their various ideas about the sun, moon, and passage of time.

In the early 1970s Myers wrote several other picture books for young readers, including *The Dragon Takes a Wife* and *How Mr. Monkey Saw the Whole World*. He was hired at the Bobbs-Merrill publishing house, and spent seven years there learning the book business from the editorial side. He went on to earn a college degree from Empire State College. His first novel for teens, *Fast Sam, Cool Clyde, and Stuff,* was published in 1975. It came about entirely by accident, thanks to a short story he had submitted to his agent, who sent it on to an editor. The editor assumed it was a chapter in a book, and when she ran into Myers at a party she asked how the rest of the project was going. As he recalled in the interview with Smith, "I said, 'It goes like this,' and I made it up on the spot. She offered me a contract."

*Fast Sam, Cool Clyde, and Stuff* tells the story of the summer when Francis, a.k.a. "Stuff," moves to 116th Street in Harlem. He and his friends, Clyde and Sam, shoot baskets and try to steer clear of the dangers on the streets. The book became a classic of young adult fiction, praised by readers for its humor, and taught in schools for its message about self-esteem and community. Myers found a steady market for his novels after that, and began publishing one every year. His 1979 title *The Young Landlords,* about a group of teens who are given an apartment building to manage on their own, was the first of his works to win a Coretta Scott King Award from the American Library Association. The annual honor is given to the top book for young readers by an African American author.

## Teen titles won devoted audience

Myers would win the King award several more times for other books. *Motown and Didi: A Love Story* was the next to earn the honor. The 1985 novel is set in Harlem, where Didi and her boyfriend, Motown, fall in love. He wants to find a good job, while Didi hopes to go to college, but their more immediate goal is to keep her brother out of trouble and away from the local drug kingpin.

Four years later, Myers won again for *Fallen Angels,* about a Harlem teen who enlists in the Army during the Vietnam War (1954–75). Myers called upon his own recollections of military service to write it, but the work was really written in honor of his younger brother, Sonny, who followed in Myers's footsteps and enlisted in the Army in 1968. Sonny was sent to Southeast Asia at the height of American involvement in the Vietnam conflict, and was killed in combat on his first day. Like most of Myers's works, it became a staple on school and public library bookshelves. Years later, he said the best letter he ever received from a reader was from a young man who had wanted to enlist in the military because of the Persian Gulf War in 1991. "He was so excited he couldn't wait until he turned 17 to join up," Myers recalled in the interview with Smith. "He read my book and changed his mind."

*Scorpions,* which also appeared in 1988, recounts the story of Jamal, a middle-schooler who unwisely accepts a gun when an older teen asks him to hold onto it for him. The plot was inspired by a true-life tale: Myers and his sons once played ball in their neighborhood park with another kid, who later disappeared. They later learned he was involved in a shooting. *Somewhere in the Darkness,* which won the King award in 1993, is a characteristic Myers tale, both in its challenging fictional premise and in the compelling story the author weaves around it. This novel involves Jimmy Little, who lives in Harlem with his foster family. His father, Crab, has just been released from prison, and arrives to take Jimmy on a road trip. On their journey down South, Jimmy begins to realize his father is fatally ill and wants to clear his name of the crime that sent him to prison.

## Collector of vintage images

Myers has written historical fiction as well as his contemporary novels for young adults. He has also written poetry and compiled photo albums that feature images of African American families over the generations. Myers collects these historical photos from rare book dealers and antiques stores during his book tours across the United States. One of these works is *One More River to Cross: An African-American Photograph Album,* which depicts families' journeys, from the slavery era to the migration to northern cities in the early years of the twentieth century. The idea for these books, Myers said, came when he was teaching writing to youngsters in a Jersey City elementary school near his home. As an assignment, he had them bring in images of their grandparents when they were children. "The kids loved the photographs," he explained to Brown. "They wanted to learn why their grandparents would wear those kinds [of] clothes, shoes, what kind of house they lived in."

Myers has worked with his son, Christopher, who illustrated *Harlem: A Poem,* another Coretta Scott King award-winner. His 1999 novel *Monster* won that award, as well as the Michael L. Printz Award, another honor from the American Library Association. *Monster* recounts the terrible chain of events that lands sixteen-year-old Steve Harmon on trial for murder. Steve, who comes from a stable household and had hoped to become a filmmaker, was asked by some tougher kids in his neighborhood to serve as lookout during a store robbery. The owner is killed, and the teens are arrested. Myers spares no detail when describing Steve's fear of being preyed upon by the veteran teen criminals with whom he is housed. Patty Campbell, in a review for *Horn Book,* compared Myers's latest work to the classics *Catcher in the Rye* by J. D. Salinger, S. E. Hinton's *The Outsiders,* and others. She asserted that Myers's "stunning new novel … joins these landmark books. Looking backward, *Monster* is the peak achievement of a career that has paralleled the growth of the genre."

Myers has written dozens of books over the years, including biographies of Malcolm X (1925–1965) and Muhammad Ali (1942–). He finally chronicled his own fascinating life story in *Bad Boy: A Memoir,* which appeared in 2002. He dedicated it to the sixth-grade teacher who found him professional help for his speech difficulty. Myers writes of his teen years in Harlem, and his flirtations with the criminal element, but also details his path to becoming a successful author. His story is all the more remarkable when he reveals that his foster father never learned to read—a discovery Myers made only after the man died. "Sometimes my father would have me read something to him," Myers wrote in his autobiography, "telling me it was because of his weak eyes." Many years later, when his father was dying, Myers gave him a book on which he and his son had collaborated, but his father never commented on it. "After his death, I went through his papers and saw the childlike scrawl that he used to fill out forms, and the misunderstandings he had of those forms.… Other correspondence indicated that his business affairs were being supervised by a friend at his job. It was then I realized that he had never commented on any of my books because he couldn't read them"

## For More Information

*Periodicals*

Brown, Jennifer M. "Walter Dean Myers Unites Two Passions." *Publishers Weekly* (March 22, 1999): p. 45.

Campbell, Patty. "*Monster.*" *Horn Book* (January 2000): p. 42.

Corbett, Sue. "Walter Dean Myers Has Been Writing Poignant, Tough Stories for and About At-Risk Kids." Knight Ridder/Tribune News Service (January 26, 2000): p. K6508.

Gallo, Don. "A Man of Many Ideas: Walter Dean Myers." *Writing!* (February-March 2004): p. 10.

Higgins, Jim. "Former 'Bad Boy' Taps into Youths' Minds, Struggles." *Milwaukee Journal Sentinel* (May 26, 2002): p. 1.

McElmeel, Sharron L. "A Profile: Walter Dean Myers." *Book Report* (September-October 2001): p. 42.

Smith, Amanda. "Walter Dean Myers: This Award-Winning Author for Young People Tells It Like It Is." *Publishers Weekly* (July 20, 1992): p. 217.

"*Somewhere in the Darkness.*" *Publishers Weekly* (March 9, 1992): p. 58.

### Web Sites

Myers, Walter Dean. "Author Studies Homepage." *Scholastic Books.* http://www2.scholastic.com/teachers/authorsandbooks/authorstudies/authorhome.jhtml?authorID=67&collateralID=5250&displayName=Biography (accessed on July 15, 2004).

# Donna Jo Napoli

U·X·L newsmakers • *volume 3*

*February 28, 1948* • *Miami, Florida*

## Author

**D**onna Jo Napoli moonlights from her job as a professor of linguistics at a Pennsylvania college to write books for children and young adults. Her stories range from magical retellings of ancient or medieval folktales, like *Zel* and *The Magic Circle,* to realistic, emotionally wrenching tales of kids confronting divorce and death in their family, such as *The Bravest Thing.* An essay on her career in the *St. James Guide to Young Adult Writers* commended Napoli's "belief in the ability of ordinary people to overcome and to survive."

## Lost home more than once

Napoli never planned to become a writer. Born in 1948, she grew up in an Italian American family in Miami, Florida, the youngest of four children. She suffered from an eye problem that was not diagnosed until she was ten, but once it was corrected, she became an avid reader. But there were still other challenges in her early life. "We had no books in the house," she recalled in an interview published on the DownHome-

Books.com Web site. "My father bought the paper—but only to read the betting sheets and any news that might affect his chances to win bets." In an article she wrote for *Horn Book* she revealed that her father was a compulsive gambler: "When he'd make money at work, he'd gamble it—sometimes completely away. Then we'd get kicked out of where we were living and my parents would fight and I'd go sit in a tree and read a book and live in the world I created inside my head."

Napoli was a talented student in her teens, and was accepted at Harvard University. During her first year there she took a required

> **"** I try hard to give my readers other places—to let them experience via my stories cultures and lands that they might not be able to experience otherwise—to give them what I sought in books. **"**

composition class, which had one fiction assignment. After her professor read the assignment, she suggested that Napoli could pursue a career as a novelist. "I decided then and there never to take another English course," she wrote in the *Horn Book* article. "I simply was not going to be lured into a vocation that was so financially unstable."

After earning an undergraduate degree in mathematics, Napoli decided to study Romance languages in graduate school. These are Italian, French, Spanish, and other languages descended from Latin. She went on to earn a doctorate from Harvard in 1973. She also spent a year studying linguistics, which is the scientific study of languages and their structure, sounds, meanings, and relation to human culture. During her college years she married and began a family that would eventually number five children.

## Math trained her to write

Napoli spent the next dozen years living and working in a number of college towns, from Northampton, Massachusetts, to Ann Arbor,

Michigan. She became a professor of linguistics at Swarthmore College in Pennsylvania in 1987, and also served as chair of its linguistics department. She is the author of five books in her professional field. Her first book for children, *The Hero of Barletta,* was published in 1988. Its story is based on an Italian folktale about a giant who works to save the village where he lives from an invading army. But Napoli's second career as a writer did not come about quickly. "I spent fourteen long years gathering letters of rejection before an editor finally bought one of my stories," she noted in the *Horn Book* article. Her early training in mathematics had served her well, she believed. "To do math problems, you have to focus and work and work.... So mathematics teaches persistence. And there may be no more important quality for a writer than persistence."

Napoli only turned to writing fiction as a second job after she experienced a personal loss. For months afterward she exchanged letters with a friend, who came to her a year later, letters in hand, and suggested they would make a terrific novel. "That's when I realized I really love to write," Napoli told an audience of young readers, according to *Winston-Salem Journal* reporter Kim Underwood. Not surprisingly, many of her books deal with a loss or challenge, and often feature characters who are coming to terms with a change or disruption in their lives. *Soccer Shock* was one of Napoli's more fantastical early works. It was also her first children's story that was not a folktale retold. Its hero is Adam, a ten-year-old who is jolted by an electric shock. As a result, his freckles now talk to him, and Adam tries to use his newfound power to become the winning athlete on his soccer team. Napoli wrote two other novels in which Adam confronts various challenges, *Shark Shock* and *Shelley Shock.*

Overcoming phobias was the theme of Napoli's 1994 book *When the Water Closes Over My Head.* Mikey, age nine, is terrified of taking swimming lessons, and his older sister teases him about it, but he eventually learns to overcome his fear. *Booklist*'s Hazel Rochman liked the fact that Napoli's characters debunked gender stereotypes— Mikey cooks better than his sister, and his little brother likes to play dress-up. When their grandmother disapproves, Mikey defends his brother. Rochman also noted the way Napoli had the characters interact at several levels, where they "bicker about breakfast cereal and also confront elemental issues of grief and rivalry and love."

## Napoli's Major Works for Young Adults

*The Magic Circle,* Dutton, 1993.

*Zel,* Dutton/Penguin, 1996.

*Song of the Magdalene,* Scholastic, 1996.

*Stones in Water,* Dutton/Penguin, 1997.

*Sirena,* Scholastic, 1998.

*Crazy Jack,* Delacorte, 1999.

*Beast,* Simon and Schuster/Atheneum, 2000.

*Three Days,* Dutton, 2001.

*Daughter of Venice,* Random/Wendy Lamb Books, 2002.

*Breath,* Simon and Schuster/Atheneum, 2003.

*The Great God Pan,* Random/Wendy Lamb Books, 2003.

Napoli also wrote about a young man with agoraphobia, or the fear of leaving one's home. The title character in *Albert* struggles to leave the house day after day, but is unable to do so. One day he sticks his hand out of the window to check the weather, and a bird begins building a nest for her eggs in it. Now he has to remain at the window day after day, but in the process he begins to observe the world outside. When the eggs hatch and the birds leave their nest, Albert realizes he, too, is ready to leave and explore the world.

## Her favorite book

Napoli has said that *The Bravest Thing,* one of her books for readers age eight to eleven, is her favorite among the works she has authored. The story deals with multiple sorrows: ten-year-old Laurel has a pet rabbit named Bun Bun who has a litter, but Bun Bun refuses to nurse her babies and they die. Laurel decides to mate her again, and the same thing happens. In the meantime, Laurel also learns her beloved aunt has cancer, and that she herself has scoliosis, or a curvature of the spine that will require her to wear a brace. Napoli's handling of the difficult subject matter, noted a reviewer for *Publishers Weekly,* "inspires the reader to believe that obstacles, no matter how daunting, can be made smaller through courage."

Napoli's five children often provided story ideas in an indirect way. One of her daughters, Eva, once asked her mother during a read-aloud moment why there were so many mean women in fairy tales. The question prompted Napoli to write *The Magic Circle,* a twist on the classic Brothers Grimm fairy tale of Hansel and Gretel. It is also the first of her books directed at young adult readers. In the original tale, two children are abandoned in the forest on the orders of their stepmother during a time of starvation in the land. They become lost but discover a delightful house made of candy. An elderly woman lures them in and feeds them lavishly, but then plans to bake them in an oven and eat them. In Napoli's story, the dreadful witch had once been a respected midwife and healer, but was condemned as a witch by her community during a wave of religious fervor in late 1600s Germany. She made a deal with the dark forces in order to save her daughter, but was tricked by them and now must live a solitary forest life. *The Magic Circle* was named Best Book of the Year in a 1993 *Publisher's Weekly* round-up, and won several other awards as well.

## Besieged medieval village

A summer spent working on a farm when her children were very young inspired some of the plot of *Breath,* Napoli's 2003 novel for young adults. The story's kernel, however, is another reworking of a classic fairy tale. In this case, the fairy tale was based on a real event: in 1284, bothered by a rat infestation, the town of Hameln, Germany, paid a musician to lead the vermin away. When the city then refused to pay the piper the money he was due, he led the town's children away, too. Napoli read about Hameln and was intrigued by the idea that the town may have experienced a bout of ergot poisoning at the time. Ergot infests stores of rye and other grains, and causes stillborn children, hallucinations, bouts of twitching, and livestock deaths. Modern historians believe the ergot poisonings brought on the odd behavior that incited witch hunts in many places throughout the ages.

*Breath* is narrated by Salz, a twelve-year-old boy who has cystic fibrosis. This is a genetic disorder that causes the lungs to fill with mucus; it has no cure and only in modern times did its sufferers live to reach adulthood. Napoli based her character on an old version of the tale, in which one boy does not go with the other children to their deaths, and hints he was left behind because he is disabled. In Napoli's story, the townspeople come to believe that Salz, who coughs incessantly, is a witch, since he has not succumbed to the strange disease that has overtaken many. This is because he has not drunk any of the beer made from the ergot-infested rye. Susan P. Bloom, reviewing *Breath* for *Horn Book,* called it an "intriguing tale" that could have stood on its own without the Pied Piper story, "so compelling are the portraits of its protagonist and family and the horrific events that beset them."

## Re-imagines fairy tales

Many of Napoli's books are retellings of classic folktales or myths. These include *Zel,* the story of Rapunzel, and *Sirena,* a romantic twist on the Sirens who were said to have lured Greek sailors to their deaths in the ancient world. *Beast* reworks the classic Beauty and the Beast story, and adds a language lesson. It begins in Persia in the 1500s, and features a prince who is turned into a lion as punishment. He makes his way to France, where he knows there is a woman, Belle, and a rose garden that will save him. "On this grueling trip the reader feels the prince's loss of humanity," noted Bloom in a *Horn Book* review. The critic also noted that the story turns compelling when Belle finds him in the abandoned castle where he is hiding. The Beast leaves it only to hunt his own food, which repulses him. "Getting past her initial fear, the courageous Belle cleans the Beast's muzzle of blood," notes Bloom, and the two read together from *The Aeneid,* an epic Latin masterpiece from the first century B.C.E. Persian, Arabic, and French words appear elsewhere in the story, and Napoli provides a glossary at the end for readers.

Napoli still teaches at Swarthmore, but also likes to visit schools and meet her young readers in person. She has written books with others, including *How Hungry Are You?* with mathematician Richard Tchen. With her son, Robert Furrow, she wrote *Sly and the Pet Mysteries,* which was published in 2004. She has also collaborated with her daughter, Eva, on *Bobby the Bonobo,* a book about a pet monkey that is scheduled for publication in 2006.

## For More Information

### Books

*St. James Guide to Young Adult Writers.* Second edition. Farmington Hills, MI: St. James Press, 1999.

### Periodicals

Bloom, Susan P. "*Beast.*" *Horn Book* (September 2000): p. 577.

Bloom, Susan P. "Donna Jo Napoli: *Breath.*" *Horn Book* (January-February 2004): p. 85.

"*The Bravest Thing.*" *Publishers Weekly* (October 30, 1995): p. 62.

DeCandido, GraceAnne A. "*The Great God Pan.*" *Booklist* (April 15, 2003): p. 1464.

Napoli, Donna Jo. " What's Math Got to Do with It?" *Horn Book* (January 2001): p. 61.

Rochman, Hazel. "*When the Water Closes over My Head.*" *Booklist* (January 1, 1994): p. 827.

Underwood, Kim. " Just Watch; Author Recommends Close Observation Followed Up with a Fertile Imagination." *Winston-Salem Journal* (November 12, 2001): p. D1.

### Web Sites

"Author interviews: September 2003: Donna Jo Napoli." *DownHomeBooks.com.* http://www.downhomebooks.com/napoli.htm (accessed on July 15, 2004).

"Biography." *Donna Jo Napoli.com.* http://www.donnajonapoli.com/biography.html (accessed on July 15, 2004).

# Gavin Newsom

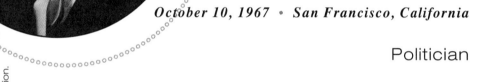

*October 10, 1967* • *San Francisco, California*

Politician

**J**ust before Valentine's Day weekend in 2004, recently elected San Francisco Mayor Gavin Newsom ordered the county clerk to begin issuing marriage licenses for same-sex couples who applied at San Francisco City Hall. Newsom's daring move allowed more than four thousand couples to get married that weekend in his city. He became a hero to the gay and lesbian community for his defiance, but he claimed he was simply acting in good conscience after President George W. Bush (1946–) criticized court challenges that had defended same-sex unions in other states. "I'd just taken an oath as mayor of the most diverse city, where people are living together and prospering together across every conceivable difference," *People* journalist J. D. Heyman quoted him as saying. "And for the President to try to deny millions of Americans the same rights that he and I have just didn't seem right."

## Suffered from dyslexia

The youngest mayor of San Francisco since 1897 was born Gavin Christopher Newsom on October 10, 1967. He was a fourth-generation San Franciscan, and came from a politically well-connected family. His grandfather was a friend of a California governor in the 1960s, and his father, William, served as a California appeals court judge for many years. Newsom's father was also a boyhood pal of one of San Francisco's richest citizens, Gordon Getty (1933–). The elder Newsom and the billionaire oil heir had known one another since their high school days in the 1940s. When a Getty grandson, Jean Paul III (1956–), was abducted by kidnappers in Italy in 1973, Newsom's

> **"My reward at the end of the day is that I can live with myself. I did my job and had a conscience. That's more powerful than being mayor."**

father and others traveled there to pay the ransom money after the teenager's ear was cut off and sent to a newspaper.

Newsom's parents had divorced by then. He and his younger sister, Hilary, were raised primarily by their mother, Tessa, although they remained close to their father and also to the Gettys. Newsom's mother worked as a bookkeeper, waitress, and secretary to make ends meet, and Newsom later admitted that his school years were difficult because of his dyslexia, a learning disorder that makes writing and spelling difficult. He went to a French-American bilingual academy, then to the Notre Dame de Victoire school in San Francisco. After graduating from Redwood High School in Marin County, he won a partial baseball scholarship to Santa Clara University, graduating in 1989 with a political science degree.

## Opened wine business

Newsom's family connections helped get him a job in the office of a well-connected San Francisco real estate mogul, but the position paid

## San Francisco's First Lady Lives in New York

San Francisco Mayor Gavin Newsom is the husband of television legal commentator Kimberly Guilfoyle Newsom. During his election campaign in 2003, she took a leave of absence from her job in the prosecutor's office in San Francisco to avoid any conflict of interest. She began appearing on CNN's *Larry King Live* as a legal commentator during episodes devoted to the case of Laci Peterson, a pregnant woman from California who disappeared on Christmas Eve in 2002.

Like her husband, Guilfoyle Newsom is a lifelong San Franciscan with Irish roots. Her Irish-born father was a cop and real estate investor, and her mother, who died when Guilfoyle Newsom was ten, was of Puerto Rican heritage. She attended the University of California's Davis campus, and then helped put herself through law school at the University of San Francisco by working as a model. After a stint in the Los Angeles District Attorney's Office, she returned to take a similar job in her hometown. She rose to national prominence in 2001, some two years before her husband, when she was assigned to a notorious dog-mauling case in which a large dog attacked Diane Whipple, a lacrosse coach. Guilfoyle Newsom won a murder conviction against Whipple's neighbors, a pair of attorneys who owned the dog.

Guilfoyle Newsom married her husband in December of 2001, when he was still serving on the San Francisco Board of Supervisors. Their wedding reception was hosted by longtime friends Gordon and Ann Getty at their art-filled home in the Pacific Heights section of the city. In January of 2004, when her husband became mayor, Guilfoyle Newsom resigned from her prosecutor's job for good. She was hired by the cable channel Court TV as the co-host of a daily trial coverage program called *Both Sides*. The job forces her to spend most of her week in New York City, and to commute in order to see her equally busy husband.

just $18,000 a year. In 1992 he and Getty's son, Billy, a friend since childhood, decided to open a wine business. They called their Fillmore Street store the PlumpJack Wine Shop. Their venture was financed by the elder Getty, and named after an opera Gordon Getty had written, based on a character from Shakespeare.

The wine store proved a success, and became the basis for an entire PlumpJack empire. They opened the PlumpJack Cafe, also on Fillmore Street, in 1993, followed by a Napa Valley winery in 1995. Their companies expanded in 1996 to include the Balboa Café and the MatrixFillmore nightclub three years later. Newsom was busy running these ventures, but agreed to host a 1995 fundraiser for San Francisco's Democratic mayoral candidate, Willie L. Brown Jr. (1934–), at one of his San Francisco venues. When Brown won the election, he gave Newsom a post as the city's parking and traffic commissioner.

In 1997 Brown named Newsom to fill a vacancy on the San Francisco Board of Supervisors, the equivalent of its city council. A year later, Newsom ran for election to keep the seat, and won. He went on to gain some notoriety in the city for a controversial ballot proposal called "Care Not Cash." For some years, the famously liberal city had been offering welfare payments to San Francisco's homeless, prompted in part by the famously high cost of housing. Newsom's bill ended the cash payments and gave the homeless vouchers for shelter, counseling, and treatment instead. The referendum passed, but was contested in the courts and later overturned.

## A heated campaign

San Francisco has term limits for mayors, and Brown was prohibited from seeking a third term in 2003. Newsom cast his hat into the ring for the mayoral race in November of 2002. The field was soon crowded with a number of other Democrats in the left-leaning city, and some of them tried to make an issue of his ties to the Getty oil fortune. But Newsom was honest in disclosing his financial records to the press, and sold his real estate development business to his father and Gordon Getty in order to avoid a conflict of interest. He also stepped away from the day-to-day management of his other ventures for the same reason. His foes painted him as a well-heeled socialite with political connections, but Newsom stressed his business experience over the last decade and promised to run City Hall the same way if elected. "I started every one of those businesses," he said in an interview with *San Francisco Chronicle* writers Chuck Finnie, Rachel Gordon, and Lance Williams. "Conceived of them, wrote the business plans, got all the investors, and by no means are the investors exclusive to the Getty family."

It was a tough campaign with several experienced opponents, but Newsom emerged as a leader as the November election date neared. Though he had a strong finish in the balloting that day, no candidate received more than fifty percent of the vote, and a run-off election was held a few weeks later. In that contest, he bested Green Party candidate Matt Gonzalez (1965–). When he was sworn in on January 8, 2004, he was just thirty-six years old. It made him the city's youngest mayor since 1897, and one of the youngest to lead a major American city at the time.

In his first weeks in office, Newsom fulfilled his campaign pledge to voters that he would be fiscally conservative in budget matters but liberal on social matters. He appointed San Francisco's first female fire chief and female police chief, and cut his own $168,900 salary by fifteen percent to help reduce a budget deficit estimated at $330 million. On January 20 he was in Washington, D.C., for President Bush's annual State of the Union address. In it, Bush condemned what he described as "activist" judges, who were undermining the Defense of Marriage Act (DOMA) passed by Congress and signed into law by President Bill Clinton in 1996. DOMA denied federal recognition of same-sex marriages, and also allowed states the right to refuse to recognize same-sex marriages that had taken place in other states. At the time, Vermont allowed same-sex unions, and in late 2003 the Massachusetts Supreme Court issued a ruling that paved the way for same-sex couples to wed in that state.

## Made International Headlines

Back home, Newsom began doing some legal research. He looked into California's Proposition 22, which state voters had approved in 2000. This law defined marriage as a contract between a man and a woman. Newsom then checked the state's constitution, which had an "equal protection" guarantee—meaning that the state's laws should apply equally to all citizens. Believing that Proposition 22 was unconstitutional in his state, he decided to challenge it. He first called California's leading Democrat politicians in Washington, who advised the new mayor against taking such a politically controversial stance.

On his thirty-sixth day in office, Newsom instructed City Hall to begin issuing marriage licenses for same-sex couples who came to apply for them. The decision was timed with what had become an annual protest by gay-rights activists at City Hall, called the "Freedom to Marry" rally. Newsom convinced two prominent activists, Del Martin, age eighty-three, and her seventy-nine-year-old partner, Phyllis Lyon, to apply for a license and become the first to marry in the city. They agreed, and it set off a rush to City Hall. Over the holiday weekend, same-sex San Franciscan couples arrived to apply for licenses, and then television news cameras from across the United States began filming the long lines of couples waiting to apply. Some

flew in from across the country, including television personality Rosie O'Donnell (1962–) and her longtime partner.

Newsom timed the event perfectly: Martin and Lyon were married on February 12, a day the courts were closed, and the next day was the start of a three-day weekend. Conservative Christian groups immediately filed motions to halt the same-sex unions, but two city judges denied their requests. The judges said it should be decided when the courts opened on the next business day. Newsom allowed City Hall to stay open round the clock through the weekend to handle the demand for marriage licenses, and many employees even volunteered their hours. By Monday, February 16, 2,340 weddings had taken place, including that of Newsom's chief of staff, as well as another involving his policy director, at which he officiated.

*Mayor Gavin Newsom stands between two newlyweds who were able to marry after the city of San Francisco, CA, began issuing marriage licenses to gay couples.* AP/Wide World Photos. Reproduced by permission.

## Challenged governor, even president

On Sunday, February 22, California Governor Arnold Schwarzenegger (1947–) told the media that Newsom had stepped out of line.

According to an article by Jeremy Quittner in the *Advocate,* Schwarzenegger said, "In San Francisco it is license for marriage of same sex. Maybe the next thing is another city that hands out licenses for assault weapons and someone else hands out licenses for selling drugs; I mean, you can't do that." On February 24 President Bush asserted that he would support a constitutional amendment prohibiting same-sex marriages in the United States.

Newsom quickly called a press conference to challenge the President's remarks. Bush has "tried to divide this country in order to advance his political career by messing with the Constitution," Newsom told reporters, according to an article by Gordon and her *San Francisco Chronicle* colleague Simone Sebastian. "I can't believe people of good conscience, from any ideological perspective, can honestly say that the Constitution should be used to take rights away from people when the Constitution was conceived to advance the rights of people in this country," Newsom asserted. "It is a terrible day because of what the president of the United States has decided to do to divide the United States of America. That, I think, is shameful." The proposed amendment to ban same-sex marriages was defeated in Congress in July of 2004.

On March 11 California Supreme Court justices ordered San Francisco to stop issuing licenses for same-sex couples. Over four thousand couples had already been wed in the city. Newsom was a hero to many, but was criticized in other quarters. Hosts of radio call-in shows and television pundit-fests condemned him, and his office received negative e-mails as well. Newsom had been termed one of the Democratic Party's most exciting new names, and had once even declared his intention to make a bid for the White House someday. Some believed he had risked his political future by supporting same-sex unions. However, his City Hall predecessor, Mayor Art Agnos (1938–), signed the first domestic partnership bill in the United States into law in 1988. Back then, Agnos was also warned against taking such a stance, but a decade later such bills were commonplace in municipalities and companies throughout the United States. Newsom has said he was merely putting his city at the forefront once again. "We will look back in 15 to 30 years in disbelief that we were ever having this kind of debate," he told Quittner. "Of that I am absolutely certain."

# For More Information

## *Periodicals*

Finnie, Chuck, Rachel Gordon, and Lance Williams. "Newsom's Portfolio; Mayoral Hopeful Has Parlayed Getty Money, Family Ties and Political Connections into Local Prominence." *San Francisco Chronicle* (February 23, 2003): p. A1.

Gordon, Rachel. "Newsom Asks: What Do You Need?; In Door-to-Door Visits, S.F. Workers Extend Helping Hand to Crime-Weary Residents." *San Francisco Chronicle* (June 11, 2004): p. A1.

Gordon, Rachel, and Simone Sebastian. "Same-Sex Marriage Ban of 'National Importance'; Feisty Mayor: Newsom Calls Bush Reaction Shameful." *San Francisco Chronicle* (February 25, 2004): p. A1.

Heyman, J. D. "The Marrying Man: San Francisco Mayor Gavin Newsom Grants Marriage Licenses to Gay Couples—And Sparks a National Movement." *People* (March 29, 2004): p. 93.

Medina, Marcy. "Pet Project. (San Francisco Prosecutor Kimberly Guilfoyle)." *WWD* (April 9, 2001): p. 16.

Murphy, Dean E. "Left Faces Left in San Francisco Runoff Vote for Mayor." *New York Times* (Dec 7, 2003): p. A26.

Quittner, Jeremy. "Gavin's Gay Gamble: Mayor Gavin Newsom Makes San Francisco a Mecca for Gay Marriage. What Was This Straight Guy Thinking?" *Advocate* (March 30, 2004): p. 28.

Said, Carolyn. "Win for Bottom Line; S.F. Mayor-Elect Brings Commercial Smarts to His Job." *San Francisco Chronicle* (December 11, 2003): p. B1.

Sandalow, Marc, and Rachel Gordon. "Newsom Now a National Figure; Same-Sex Marriage Decision Turns Him into Lightning Rod." *San Francisco Chronicle* (Feb 29, 2004): p. A1.

Taylor, Chris. "I Do … No, You Don't! Why San Francisco's Brash Mayor Is Taking on Schwarzenegger and Bush over Gay Marriage." *Time* (March 1, 2004): p. 40.

Zinko, Carolyne. "A Wedding to Remember; Newsom-Guilfoyle Nuptials Talk of the Town." *San Francisco Chronicle* (December 16, 2001): p. E5.

# Jenny Nimmo

*January 15, 1942* • *Windsor, Berkshire, England*

## Writer

**B**ritish author Jenny Nimmo writes about spell-casting cats and youngsters who inherit magical powers. The author of more than four dozen books for children and young-adult readers, Nimmo did not begin writing in earnest until she became a mother, though she had always written far-fetched, sometimes gory tales when she was in her teens. "A lot of people, my teachers particularly, used to throw my books back at me and tell me not to write such rubbish," she once recalled in an interview that appeared on the HarperCollins Web site. "I took them at their word and I stopped writing. Perhaps if I'd persevered then I might have started writing earlier, but I didn't have the confidence."

## Sent to boarding school

Nimmo has lived in Wales for years, and some of her best-known fiction draws upon ancient Welsh legends. But she is English by birth, a native of the Berkshire district, where she was born in 1942. An only

U·X·L newsmakers • volume 3

child, she was sent to live with relatives after her physicist-father died when she was five. Her uncle, who ran a free-range chicken farm, taught her to read, with the help of her favorite book at the time, *The Bear That Never Was*. As she remembered in the HarperCollins interview: "It was about a bear who comes out of hiding and is put to work in a factory because no-one believes that he is a bear, they all think he's a silly man who doesn't want to work! That was the book that taught me how to read."

Around the age of nine, Nimmo was sent to a boarding school. Teachers there encouraged her talent for drama, and she also developed

> **"Her writing is powerful and as musical as the Welsh culture about which she is writing."**
>
> *St. James Guide to Fantasy Writers*

musical abilities. She remained a voracious reader. When she read through the entire library at her middle school, she was given special permission to check out books from the high-school library shelves. It was during this time that she began writing her own murder-mystery stories that her teachers criticized. After leaving school, Nimmo put her dramatic skills to use by working with the Theatre Southeast, a company in Sussex and Kent counties. She appeared in its productions and also served as an assistant stage manager for three years.

In 1963, Nimmo took off for Amalfi, Italy, a picturesque Mediterranean coastal area south of Naples. She worked as a governess there for a year, teaching English to a family of Italian youngsters. When she returned to England, she landed a job with the television production arm of the British Broadcasting Corporation (BBC) in London. She worked as a photographic researcher for two years, and then served as an assistant floor manager for a time. In 1970, she became a director and writer on the staff of a long-running BBC children's program, *Jackanory*. It was one of the most popular children's television shows in British history, featuring tales told by well-known stage and screen personalities. Nimmo's job as a writer was to adapt children's books for its teleplay format.

## Major Works by Nimmo

*The Bronze Trumpeter,* Angus & Robertson, 1975.

*The Snow Spider,* Methuen, 1986, Dutton, 1987.

*Emlyn's Moon,* Methuen, 1987, published as *Orchard of the Crescent Moon,* Dutton, 1989.

*The Chestnut Soldier,* Methuen, 1989, Dutton, 1991.

*Ultramarine,* Methuen, 1990, Dutton, 1992.

*Delilah and the Dogspell,* Methuen, 1991.

*Rainbow and Mr. Zed,* Methuen, 1992, Dutton, 1994.

*The Stone Mouse,* Walker, 1993.

*The Witch's Tears,* Collins, 1996.

*Gwion and the Witch,* Pont Books, 1996.

*Seth and the Strangers,* Mammoth, 1997.

*The Dragon's Child,* Hodder & Stoughton, 1997.

*Delilah Alone,* Mammoth, 1997.

*Toby in the Dark,* Walker, 1999.

*Esmeralda and the Children Next Door,* Methuen, 1999, Houghton, 2000.

*Something Wonderful,* Collins, Harcourt, 2001.

*Midnight for Charlie Bone,* Egmont, Orchard, 2002.

*Beak and Whisker,* Egmont, 2002.

*Invisible Vinnie,* Corgi, 2003.

## Imagined a talking statue

Nimmo thought of her own idea for a story, based on her time in Italy, about a statue that comes to life in the garden of a villa. As she recalled in the HarperCollins interview, she decided to "set it in Sicily in 1915, during the First World War. I gave it to my producer and she said that it was, 'No good for television but it would make a wonderful book. Go away and lengthen it, make it into a full-length novel' and so I did." *The Bronze Trumpeter* was published in 1975 to some excellent reviews. Its plot centers on a young boy who is befriended by the statue of a musician on the grounds of a Sicilian villa that comes to life for him. The lonely boy learns much from his friendship with the Trumpeter, who even helps him uncover a scheme cooked up by his frosty governess, Fraulein Helga.

But Nimmo would not publish another book for almost a decade. In 1974, she married artist and illustrator David Wynn Millward, and soon began a family that would number three children. They settled in Wales, and Nimmo did not begin writing again until her youngest child began preschool. She wrote a children's book titled

*Tatty Apple,* about a boy named Owen and his green-and-brown rabbit, Tatty Apple, who has magical powers.

In 1986, Nimmo earned terrific reviews for her next book, *The Snow Spider,* which also became the first of an acclaimed fantasy-fiction trilogy of the same name. The young-adult novel won the Tir na n-Og Award for best children's book either in the Welsh language or set in Wales, given by the Welsh Books Council the following year. It borrowed many elements from an old Welsh saga, the *Mabinogion,* for the modern-day plot. The *Mabinogion* dated back to the medieval era, but its tales were thought by scholars to be even hundreds of years older than that. Its intertwined stories involved princes, far-off lands, magical spells, and giants.

## Boy struggles with powers

*The Snow Spider* chronicled the tale of Gwyn Griffiths, a ten-year-old boy in Wales whose sister has recently disappeared while walking in the hilly Welsh countryside. She is presumed dead. Gwyn's mother is grief-stricken, and his father blames him for the loss. But Gwyn's wise grandmother gives him five odd gifts for his birthday: a brooch, a pipe, some seaweed, the broken figurine of a horse, and a scarf his sister once wore. These items help him uncover his magician's gifts. It turns out that Gwyn is the descendant of Gwydion, a powerful magician, but the family's gifts have grown weaker over the generations. Gwyn's grandmother wants to help him unlock his secret talents. He tosses the brooch, for instance, and it returns to him as Arianwen, a silver spider. Arianwen becomes his helpmate, and shows him how to make contact with his sister, who may not really be dead at all.

Nimmo continued the saga of Gwyn in *Emlyn's Moon,* which was published in the United States as *Orchard of the Crescent Moon.* Its plot revolves around his neighbor and friend, Nia, who hopes to rescue her friend, Emlyn. Along the way, Gwyn learns that he and Emlyn are cousins, but the branches of their families have a long-standing grudge against one another involving Emlyn's mother, who vanished many years before.

The last of Nimmo's trilogy is *The Chestnut Soldier,* which features Gwyn on the verge of turning fourteen. He has learned much about his powers over the years, but fails to use them wisely at times.

One of his decisions puts a soldier in danger. The man has returned to the village to recuperate, after serving with the British army in Northern Ireland. In this final work, which features an epic struggle between the forces of light and dark, Gwyn finally unlocks the riddle of the broken-horse statue. An essay in the *St. James Guide to Fantasy Writers* called this trio of books "a stunning achievement. Nimmo explores Gwyn's dual existence as ancient magician and young boy through five years, by turns showing his enthusiasm and weariness for his role as his awareness grows, and also his final acceptance of what he is."

## Wrote underwater mystery

Nimmo returned to the fantasy/psychological-thriller format for teen readers with *Ultramarine* in 1990. In it, a brother and sister are sent to stay with older relatives they've never met. The seashore visit uncovers many intriguing stories about Ned and Nell's family, including the events surrounding their mother's death by drowning. They also come to realize that their real father may have been a mysterious sea creature known as a kelpie, a shape-shifting water devil of Gaelic lore who takes the shape of a horse to lure its victims. But their father tried to use his powers for good, by serving as a protector for other sea creatures. Ned and Nell learn some of this when they befriend a local eccentric who also rescues sea creatures. In the end, Ned departs for his other home—underwater. Nell's story continues solo in *Rainbow and Mr. Zed,* which finds her living with her aunt and grandmother. "Rainbow," it turns out, is Nell's real name, while Mr. Zed—"zed" is British English for "zero"—is the wicked uncle who hopes to use Nell's powers to further his own ambitions.

Talking animals, whether stuffed, stone, or real, always seem to appear in many of Nimmo's books. These include *The Stone Mouse,* in which a brother and sister discover a talking stone mouse. She has also written a comical series beginning with *Delilah and the Dogspell* in 1991. It features a spell-casting cat who uses her powers to harass the local dogs. A 1994 book, *Griffin's Castle,* features a plot that involves the carved animals decorating the walls of Wales's famed Cardiff Castle. Dinah is upset about her mother's plan to sell their old house, and asks the animals to help her thwart the plan. *Toby in the Dark,* published in 1999, is a teddy bear who helps the three children living in the home of a mean-spirited foster parent. Family strife also runs through Nimmo's books. The plot of *Milo's Wolves,* which appeared in 2001, begins when a father confesses to his three children that they have a brother, Gwendal, who has been in a clinic for many years, but is now coming home.

## More tales of magic

Nimmo began another series in 2002, "The Children of the Red King." It kicked off with *Midnight for Charlie Bone,* about a ten-year-old who discovers that he has inherited supernatural powers, and is sent off to a special academy to refine them. The series had echoes of the successful "Harry Potter" books by British author J. K. Rowling, but Charlie, unlike Harry, possesses the unique gift of being able to look at a photograph and suddenly hear the conversations and thoughts that took place at the time it was taken. The series continued with *Charlie Bone and the Time Twister* and *Charlie Bone and the Invisible Boy.*

Not all of Nimmo's books have appeared in print outside of Great Britain. Her popular "Snow Spider" and "Charlie Bone" series, as well as the two Ultramarine books and *Griffin's Castle,* have been published for American readers. Other works issued by New York City publishing houses have been *Esmeralda and the Children Next Door,* about the star in a family of circus performers, little Esmeralda, who possesses a super-strength that is a hit with audiences but embarrasses her in real life. Other children tease her because she can lift both her parents and carry them around. In *Something Wonderful,* Little Hen is a shy, hesitant hen that is the runt of her farm. Dejected when she learns she cannot take part in a special competition for the other chickens, she finds some eggs in the woods that have been accidentally left behind by the others. She stays with them until they are hatched, even braving a storm, and returns with the baby chicks to the farm and a hero's welcome. "Youngsters will enjoy and identify with this story about one small animal's special gift," noted a *School Library Journal* review from Anne Parker.

Nimmo's children are grown now, but she remains busy at her home in Llangynyw, which is named Henllan Mill. She and her husband run a summer art academy which includes lodgings and meals. She finds it hard to write during these weeks when the guest-students are around, but described it as a kind of vacation from the necessary discipline of being a full-time writer. "It's a mental break I suppose," she said in the interview that appeared on the HarperCollins Web site, "which is sometimes a good thing."

## For More Information

### Books

*St. James Guide to Fantasy Writers.* Detroit, MI: St. James Press, 1996.

### Periodicals

"Children's Notes." *Publishers Weekly* (July 12, 2004): p. 65.

Parker, Anne. *"Something Wonderful."* *School Library Journal* (September 2001): p. 202.

### Web Sites

"Authors ... An Interview with Jenny Nimmo." *HarperCollins.* http://www. harpercollins.co.uk/authors/interview.aspx?id=495&aid=4283 (accessed on July 26, 2004).

"Nimmo, Jenny." *Contemporary Authors Online.* http://web1.infotrac.gale group.com/itw/infomark/313/94/49940612w1/purl=rc1_CA_0_H1000 073184&dyn=8!xrn_3_0_H1000073184?sw_aep=itsbtrial (accessed on July 26, 2004).

# Indra K. Nooyi

*October 28, 1955 • Madras, India*

## Executive

Indra K. Nooyi is the president and chief financial officer of PepsiCo. Best known for its Pepsi soft drinks, the international powerhouse that Nooyi oversees is actually one of the world's largest snack-food companies. Its makes and sells dozens of other products, including Doritos-brand chips, the Tropicana juice line, and Quaker Oats cereals. Nooyi is one of the top female executives in the United States, and is also believed to be the highest-ranking woman of Indian heritage in corporate America.

## Joined Rock Band

Nooyi was born in Madras, India, in 1955, and was a bit of a rule breaker in her conservative, middle-class world as she grew up. In an era in India where it was considered unseemly for young women to exert themselves, she joined an all-girls' cricket team. She even played guitar in an all-female rock band while studying at Madras Christian

College. After earning her undergraduate degree in chemistry, physics, and math, she went on to enroll in the Indian Institute of Management in Calcutta. At the time, it was one of just two schools in the country that offered a master's in business administration degree, or M.B.A.

Nooyi's first job after earning her degree was with Tootal, a British textile company. It had had been founded in Manchester, England, in 1799, but had extensive holdings in India. After that, Nooyi was hired as a brand manager at the Bombay offices of Johnson & Johnson, the personal-care products maker. She was given the Stayfree account, which might have proved a major challenge for

## "Behind my cool logic lies a very emotional person."

even an experienced marketing executive. The line had just been introduced on the market in India, and struggled to create an identity with its target customers. "It was a fascinating experience because you couldn't advertise personal protection in India," she recalled in an interview with the *Financial Times*'s Sarah Murray.

Nooyi began to feel that perhaps she was underprepared for the business world. Determined to study in the United States, she applied to and was accepted by Yale University's Graduate School of Management in New Haven, Connecticut. Much to her surprise, her parents agreed to let her move to America. The year was 1978. "It was unheard of for a good, conservative, south Indian Brahmin girl to do this," she explained to Murray in the *Financial Times*. "It would make her an absolutely unmarriageable commodity after that."

## Could Not Afford Suit

Nooyi quickly settled into her new life, but struggled to make ends meet over the next two years. Though she received financial aid from Yale, she also had to work as an overnight receptionist to make ends meet. "My whole summer job was done in a sari because I had no

## Pepsi v. Coke

The rivalry between Pepsi, the flagship product of Indra Nooyi's company, and its Atlanta, Georgia-based competitor, Coca-Cola, is one of corporate America's longest-running marketing battles. In the United States alone, the soft-drink industry is a $60 billion one, with the average American consuming a staggering fifty-three gallons of carbonated soft drinks every year.

The battle between Coke and Pepsi dates back almost as long as each company's history. Both emerged as key players in early decades of the twentieth century, when soft drinks first came on the market in the United States. In the 1920s, Coca-Cola began moving aggressively into overseas markets, and even opened bottling plants near to places where U.S. service personnel were stationed during World War II. Pepsi only moved into international territory in the 1950s, but scored a major coup in 1972 when it inked a deal with the Soviet Union. With this deal, Pepsi became the first Western product ever sold to Soviet consumers.

The battle for market share heated up after 1975, when both companies stepped up their already lavishly financed marketing campaigns to win new customers. Pepsi's standard cola products had a slightly sweeter taste, which prompted one of the biggest corporate-strategy blunders in U.S. business history: in 1985, Coca-Cola launched "New Coke," which had a slightly sweeter formulation. Coke consumers were outraged. The old formula was still available under the name "Coca-Cola Classic," but the New Coke idea was quickly shelved. This incident is often studied by business-school curriculums in the United States and elsewhere, along with many other aspects of what is known as "the cola wars."

Coke is the leader in market share for carbonated colas, but soft drinks remain its core business. Pepsi, on the other hand, began acquiring other businesses in 1965 when it bought the Texas-based Frito-Lay company, and has a larger stake in the food industry.

money to buy clothes," she told Murray. Even when she went for an interview at the prestigious business-consulting firms that hired business-school students, she wore her sari, since she could not afford a business suit. Recalling that the Graduate School of Management required all first-year students to take—and pass—a course in effective communications, she said in the *Financial Times* interview that what she learned in it "was invaluable for someone who came from a culture where communication wasn't perhaps the most important aspect of business at least in my time."

Nooyi did not earn a second M.B.A. from Yale. Instead, her degree was a master of public and private management, which she finished in 1980. After commencement, she went to work at the Boston Consulting Group, a prestigious consulting firm. For the next six years she worked on a variety of international corporate-strategy projects, and went over to Motorola in 1986 as a senior executive. She remained there for four years, leaving in 1990 to join Asea Brown Boveri Inc. as its head of strategy. ABB, as the company was known, was a $6 billion Swiss-Swedish conglomerate that made industrial equipment and constructed power plants around the world.

Nooyi's skill in helping ABB find its direction in North America came to the attention of Jack Welch, the head of General Electric. He offered her a job in 1994, but so did PepsiCo chief executive officer Wayne Calloway. As she told a writer for *Business Week,* the two men knew one another, but Calloway made an appealing pitch for Nooyi's talent. He told her, she recalled, that "'Welch is the best CEO I know.... But I have a need for someone like you, and I would make PepsiCo a special place for you.'"

Nooyi chose the soft-drink maker, and became its chief strategist. Soon, she was urging PepsiCo to reshape its brand identity and assets, and became influential in a number of important decisions. She was also a lead negotiator on the high-level deals that followed. The company decided to spin off its restaurant division in 1997, for example, which made its KFC, Pizza Hut, and Taco Bell holdings into a separate company. She also looked at the successful plan by Pepsi rival Coca-Cola, which had sold of its bottling operations a decade earlier, and had been rewarded with impressive profit margins on its stock performance. Pepsi followed suit, and the 1999 initial public offering of the Pepsi bottling operations was valued at $2.3 billion. The company kept a large share of stock in it, however.

## Pointed Pepsi in the Right Direction

At PepsiCo, Nooyi has been the chief dealmaker for two of its most important acquisitions: she put together the $3.3 billion-dollar-deal for the purchase of the Tropicana orange-juice brand in 1998, and two years later was part of the team that secured Quaker Oats for $14 billion. That became one of the biggest food deals in corporate history, and added a huge range of cereals and snack-food products to the PepsiCo empire. She also helped acquire the edgy beverage maker SoBe for $337 million, and her deal beat the one submitted by Coca-Cola.

*Indra Nooyi (left) and other Pepsi-Co and Quaker Oats executives pose with products from both companies. PepsiCo purchased Quaker Oaks in 2001.* AP/Wide World Photo. Reproduced by permission.

For her impressive dealmaking talents, Nooyi was promoted to the job of chief financial officer at PepsiCo in February of 2000. It made her the highest-ranking Indian-born woman among the ranks of corporate America. A year later, she was given the title of president as well, when her longtime colleague, Steven S. Reinemund, advanced to the position of board chair and chief executive officer. Reinemund had said he would only take the job only if Nooyi came onboard as his second in command. "'I can't do it unless I have you with me,'" she recalled him telling her, according to *Business Week*.

Upon taking over as president and chief financial officer in May of 2001, Nooyi worked to keep the company on track with her vision: "For any part of the day we will have a little snack for you," she told *Business Week* in 2001. The company sold a dazzling range of snack foods and beverages, from Mountain Dew to Rice-a-Roni, from Captain Crunch cereal to Gatorade-brand sports drinks. It also owned the makers of Doritos-brand snacks and Aquafina bottled water.

## One of Corporate America's Top Visionaries

Nooyi's success in the business world landed her on *Time* magazine's list of "Contenders" for its Global Business Influentials rankings in 2003. Many watchers predict that she will someday head one of the company's divisions, such as Frito-Lay, or its core brand, PepsiCo

Beverages North America. In early 2004, there were mentions in the press that Nooyi, who still wears the occasional sari to work, was being considered for the top job at the Gucci Group, but she denied rumors that she had been talking with the Italian luxury-goods giant.

Nooyi serves on the board of trustees at the Yale Corporation, the governing board of Yale University. She lives in Greenwich, Connecticut, not far from PepsiCo's headquarters across the state line in Purchase, New York. At home, she maintains a *puja,* or traditional Hindu shrine, and once she flew to Pittsburgh after a tough session with Quaker Oats executives to pray at a shrine there to her family's deity. Her predictions that her American graduate education would hamper her marriage prospects proved untrue, for she married an Indian man, Raj, who works as a management consultant. They have two daughters who are nearly a decade apart in ages, and Nooyi occasionally brings her younger child to work. The former rock guitarist is still known to take the stage at company functions to sing. Her job, however, remains a top priority. She watches championship-game replays of the Chicago Bulls to study teamwork concepts, for example, and admitted to *Forbes* journalist Melanie Wells that she strategizes 24-7 sometimes. "I wake up in the middle of the night," she told the magazine, "and write different versions of PepsiCo on a sheet of paper."

## For More Information

*Periodicals*

Kretchmar, Laurie. "Indra K. Nooyi, 35." *Fortune* (May 6, 1991): p. 112.

Murray, Sarah. "From Poor Indian Student to Powerful US Businesswoman." *Financial Times* (January 26, 2004): p. 3.

"Nooyi Denies Gucci Talks." *WWD* (February 27, 2004): p. 2.

Pandya, Meenal. "No Going Back: Indian Immigrant Women Shape a New Identity." *World and I* (May 2001): p. 204.

"A Potent Ingredient in Pepsi's Formula." *Business Week* (April 10, 2000): p. 180.

"The Power of Two at Pepsi." *Business Week* (January 29, 2001): p. 102.

Thottam, Jyoti. "The 'Iron Woman' Is Ready to Rock." *Time* (December 1, 2003): p. 73.

"A Touch of Indigestion." *Business Week* (March 4, 2002): p. 66.

Wells, Melanie. "A General in Waiting?" *Forbes* (January 20, 2003): p. 74.

# Mary-Kate and Ashley Olsen

## Mary-Kate Olsen

*June 13, 1986 •*
*Sherman Oaks, California*

Entertainer

## Ashley Olsen

*June 13, 1986 • Sherman Oaks, California*

Entertainer

**T**wins Mary-Kate and Ashley Olsen have been in front of the cameras since before they could walk or talk. With a career that began on television in 1987, the Olsens went on to star in their own series of video movies, which sold millions of copies each and gave them a devoted fan base among American girls aged four to fourteen. They created a brand identity for themselves, and oversaw an empire that ranged from their own magazine to "marykateandashley" toothpaste long before they took their college-board exams. Each has an estimated net worth of $150 million, but both remained modest about the subject of their wealth. "That's not interesting to us," Mary-Kate told *CosmoGirl!* writer Lauren Brown. "Because we would never be like, 'Oh yeah, we're worth such-and-such.' If we don't care, no one else should."

## Their first and only audition

The Olsen twins' birthday is a well-known one: June 13, 1986. Ashley was born first, followed a few minutes later by Mary-Kate. They grew up in Sherman Oaks, California, in the San Fernando Valley, and had an older brother, Trent. Their father, Dave, worked as a mortgage banker, and their mother, Jarnette, had once danced with the Los Angeles Ballet corps. One day, their mother met a friend's friend, who was a casting agent, and mentioned that she had twin daughters. The agent asked to see a photograph, and then arranged an audition for the girls for a new ABC sitcom called *Full House*. Because child-labor laws restrict the amount of hours a minor may work, television series or films often hire a set of identical twins so that the production schedule can continue along uninterrupted. The Olsens were not identical twins but rather fraternal, but they looked enough alike to win the job.

> **"If we feel strongly enough to say no to something, then that's what happens. It's our line, it's our names and our brand—it's coming from us, Mary-Kate and Ashley. I've learned that 'No' is a full sentence."**
>
> **Mary-Kate Olsen, *CosmoGirl!*, May 2003.**

*Full House* first aired in September of 1987, and the reviews were not kind. The show starred Bob Saget as a recent widower with a large brood; his brother-in-law and a friend move in to help out. The twins were cast as Michelle Tanner, the youngest member of the household, and the Olsens' first on-screen appearance came when John Stamos, who played the friend, Jesse, carried one of them into the room. No one remembers which twin it was that day.

During the first two years on the air, *Full House* did not even make it into the Top 30 list of most-watched television shows. By the 1989–90 season, however, it did, and climbed to the No. 14 spot the next year. It peaked at No. 7 by the end of the 1991–92 season. Little Michelle's cuteness factor seemed to boost the show's popularity, but the Olsens' parents were still show-business novices. The twins were still earning Screen Actors' Guild "scale," or minimum wages, which amounted to about $4,000 per episode. Reportedly, parents of other children who were on the show suggested they negotiate for a higher fee. Dave and Jarnette found an entertainment lawyer, Robert Thorne, who had cut deals for pop superstar Prince, and he got them a higher rate.

## Made 48 hit video movies

Thorne wound up becoming the Olsen's agent, and later their business manager. He suggested they branch out with a pop record, *Brother for Sale,* which was released in 1992. A television movie, *To Grandmother's House We Go,* was also released in 1992. It was an adventure yarn set during the Christmas holidays. As the twins' popularity and star-potential increased, Thorne created the Dualstar Entertainment Group in 1993 to manage their careers. *To Grandmother's House* was followed by a slew of other films, nearly four dozen in all, that went directly to video as planned. Nearly all of them caught on with the legions of young girls who were the Olsens' most devoted fan base, the four-to-ten-year-old set. Then their fan base began to grow up along with them, and in some cases the later movies like *Passport to Paris* and *Our Lips Are Sealed* were among the top-selling titles that year on the kids' video charts.

The Olsens' first feature film, *It Takes Two,* grossed $19 million at the box office in 1995, but took in almost four times that in video sales. *Full House* ended its eight-season run that same year, and the twins remained off the small screen until ABC gave them their own short-lived sitcom, *Two of a Kind,* in 1998. Meanwhile, their multimedia empire continued to expand. Offers came pouring in, when executives of other companies began to realize that nearly anything that had their name and image would sell, and usually sell very well. A series of Olsen twins adventure novels, published by Scholastic, sold in the millions, and they also branched out into a clothing line, introduced at Wal-Mart in 2001. When Mattel began selling a line of Mary-Kate and Ashley dolls, only the company's flagship product, Barbie, outsold them.

The Olsens had become immensely rich even before they entered their teens. At the age of ten, they were the youngest millionaires in America whose wealth had not been inherited. They began to receive executive-producer credit on their films, and usually worked about five months of the year. The rest was spent at a private school in the Los Angeles area. In press interviews, they stressed that they led average lives and liked to take part in the same activities—sleepovers, horseback riding, dance classes—as their friends and fans. Their life was not without stress, however: in the mid-1990s, their parents divorced. The girls, their brother, Trent, and younger sister, Lizzie, divided their time between both parents' homes, but reportedly only one of them attended the ceremony when their father remarried.

## In the spotlight

In 2003, Mary-Kate and Ashley began their senior year of high school. It was also their most profitable year to date, with their clothing lines at Wal-Mart and related ventures bringing in $1 billion in sales at cash registers across America. Their official Web site received about two billon hits annually, and a slew of other Web sites were devoted to their stardom. Surprisingly, the twins also found a new group of fans as they grew into young adults: teenaged boys and young men. Even business journalists began to profile the duo and their company, Dualstar, and the fact that long before they had earned their high-school diplomas, each had an estimated net worth of $150 million. Thorne, who ran their company, confirmed reports that both Mary-Kate and Ashley were actively involved in every aspect of their business. They signed off on each item in the clothing line, for example. As Thorne told *People*'s Michelle Tauber, "It's always two calls" he needed to make for any deal. "And I very rarely get, 'Let my sister handle that.' They're equally voracious to know what the company is up to."

The Olsens have been described as one of just a handful of child stars who managed to maintain their appeal as they grew up. Their access to the media had been strictly controlled, but that began to change after they earned their drivers' licenses and received matching Range Rover sport-utility vehicles for their sixteenth birthdays. The twins also seemed inseparable, and many wondered if they would head to different colleges in the fall of 2004. They both chose New York University, and readied for the school year by purchasing a four-bedroom apartment in the West Village for $3 million. Both noted that they would concentrate on their academic careers for the next few years, putting their other activities on hold.

*Mary Kate (right) and Ashley Olsen in a movie still from* **New York Minute** *(2004).* © Warner Bros./ Zuma/Corbis.

In the lead-up to that, however, the Olsens had a memorable rush of PR buzz in the spring of 2004, both good and bad. Their long-awaited next feature film, *New York Minute,* tanked at the box office, and was drubbed by critics. They graduated from high school on June 7, and turned eighteen six days later, but there were reports that only Ashley had been seen with friends at the Beverly Hills Hotel pool that day. She then reportedly headed to Mexico with pals for a celebratory vacation jaunt.

## Rumors of drug abuse

Days later, the news broke that Mary-Kate's father had forced her into a treatment center just before she turned eighteen, when he could still legally do so. It was described as a "health-related" disorder, which seemed to confirm rumors over the past few months that the darker-haired Olsen twin was suffering from an eating disorder. Both twins are thin, but a backless dress Mary-Kate wore to one well-photographed event that spring revealed a near-skeletal frame. Other reports surfaced that Mary-Kate had a drug problem, especially when it was learned she had entered the Cirque Lodge in Sundance, Utah, a drug- and alcohol-abuse treatment facility. But company executives, the Olsen family, and even Ashley herself denied the cocaine-addiction rumors. She was released from the facility in late July, reportedly six pounds heavier.

Mary-Kate and Ashley were looking forward to their new college adventures in New York City. Mary-Kate was considering fine arts as possible major, while Ashley was leaning toward studying psychology. There had been fears that their Scholastic Aptitude Test (SAT) scores would be leaked to the press, but they had remained sealed. They did reveal to *People,* however, the topics of their admissions essays. Mary-Kate had explored "a big fear that I have. It was a lyric by Ben Harper that said, 'When you have everything, you have everything to lose.'" Ashley used a work by the late Abstract Expressionist painter Jackson Pollock to discuss her outlook on life for her essay, especially her life in the spotlight for the past eighteen years. The dense color swirls of Pollock's *Number 1,* she explained to Tauber in the same article, allowed the viewer "to get exactly what you want out of it, and it's kind of like our life has been, being in the public eye. People can judge it whatever way they want."

## For More Information

### *Periodicals*

Bowers, Katherine. "Take Two: The Olsens Grow Up; Mary-Kate and Ashley Have Come a Long Way Since 'Full House.'" *WWD* (September 19, 2002): p. S6.

Brown, Lauren. "Mary-Kate and Ashley." *CosmoGirl!* (May 2003): p. 136.

Brown, Scott. "Tween Queens: Wonder Twins Mary-Kate and Ashley Olsen Use Their Cuteness Powers to Achieve World Domination." *Entertainment Weekly* (November 24, 2000): p. 52.

Corliss, Richard. "Olsens in Bid to Buy Disney: Actually, No. But at 17, the TV Twins Are Powerful, Rich and the Stars of Their Very Own, Very Bad Movie." *Time* (May 17, 2004): p. 78.

David, Grainger. "The Human Truman Show: The Olsen Twins Were Born on TV 16 Years Ago. Now They're Worth More than You." *Fortune* (July 8, 2002): p. 96.

Kennedy, Dana. "Twin Peaks: Since Leaving 'Full House,' the Olsens Have Spun Their Cute Shtick into a Showbiz Empire. Is It Too Much Too Soon?" *Entertainment Weekly* (May 17, 1996): p. 38.

Louie, Rebecca. "Twin Tycoons Are Worth $300 Million—And They're Just 17." *New York Daily News* (November 24, 2003).

Ramsay, Carolyn. "The Olsens Inc." *Los Angeles Times* (January 30, 2000).

Rich, Joshua. "Twins Peaked? Tween Queens Mary-Kate and Ashley Olsen Cope with a Box Office Dud." *Entertainment Weekly* (May 21, 2004): p. 8.

"Sister To Sister: While Her Sister Mary-Kate Battles an Eating Disorder, Ashley Olsen Pledges Her Support and Talks About the Twins' Plans for the Future." *People* (July 12, 2004): p. 19.

Tauber, Michelle. "Two Cool: Boyfriends. Parties. Money. College. America's most Famous Freshmen-to-Be, Mary-Kate and Ashley Olsen, Talk Candidly About Becoming Adults—And Making the Move from Tween Queens to Movie Stars." *People* (May 3, 2004): p. 108.

"Twins Peak: Ashley & Mary-Kate Are the City's Hot New Sister Act." *New York Post* (April 15, 2004): p. 65.

Udovitch, Mim. "The Olsen Juggernaut." *New York Times Magazine* (May 27, 2001): p. 22.

# OutKast

## André Benjamin (André 3000)
*May 27, 1975* • *Georgia*

Musician

## Antwan "Big Boi" Patton
*February 1, 1975* • *Savannah, Georgia*

Musician

**O**utKast's exuberant, infectious single "Hey Ya!" helped push sales of their 2003 release *Speakerboxxx/The Love Below* past the three-million mark. This Atlanta, Georgia-raised duo, who use the professional tags "André 3000" and "Big Boi," are rap music's most unusual set of collaborators. While André 3000 favors outrageous outfits and listens to jazz, Big Boi remains more of the old-school style of rap megastar. Their dual personalities were showcased on *Speakerboxxx/The Love Below,* which was actually a pair of solo records. It became one of the top-selling records of 2003, and also won them the Grammy Award for album of the year.

## Making music in high school

OutKast met as high school students in Atlanta. "André 3000" was born André Benjamin in 1975. His father, Lawrence Walker, was a collections agent, while his mom, Sharon Benjamin Hodo, sold real estate. Antwan "Big Boi" Patton was the same age, and the son of a Marine Corps officer dad and a mother who worked as a retail supervisor. Both enrolled at Tri-Cities High School in East Point, Georgia, a school geared toward students hoping for a career in the performing arts. They stood out from the other students, they recalled, initially because of their unusually preppy clothing choices. It was music, however, that cemented their early friendship: both were fans of the more daring vein of hip-hop artists, such as De La Soul, the Brand Nubians, and A Tribe Called Quest; they also loved 1970s funk from the likes of George Clinton and Sly and the Family Stone.

> **"We're from the hood, but that's not where our music stayed."**
>
> **André Benjamin, *New York Times*, September 7, 2003.**

Benjamin and Patton began writing their own raps, which they turned into mix tapes. They initially named their outfit "2 Shades Deep," but learned it had already been taken by another group. They renamed themselves the Misfits, which they also discovered was being used. Looking up "misfit" in the dictionary, they found the synonym "outcast," and decided to use that but keep the dictionary's phonetic "k" spelling.

Benjamin and Patton admitted later to having a bit of a wild streak as teens, and Benjamin dropped out of Tri-Cities High after his junior year. Their ambitions were strong, however, and they looked for a way into the music business. They found it when they met an Atlanta-area production team, Organized Noize, which had worked in-studio with TLC to produce their hit 1994 single "Waterfalls."

## Debut single went to number 1

OutKast's first single, "Player's Ball," was released as a cassette single on LaFace Records in 1993, and on vinyl the next year. The record climbed to the top of the Billboard rap singles chart and stayed at No. 1 for six weeks. They became the first hip-hop act signed to LaFace,

## Rosa Parks vs. OutKast

OutKast has the dubious distinction of being sued by American civil-rights heroine Rosa Parks (1913–). The first single from their 1998 release *Aquemini* bore her name, though its lyrics did not mention her. Its chorus referred to her historic 1955 refusal to move to the back of a Montgomery, Alabama bus, where African Americans were expected to sit, which sparked a year-long bus boycott and virtually launched the civil-rights era in the United States. OutKast's song is about the entertainment industry, but its lyrics urge, "A-ha, hush that fuss/Everybody move to the back of the bus."

Parks sued in federal court, naming André ("André 3000") Benjamin, Antwan ("Big Boi") Patton, and their label, Arista, in her suit. Her lawyers argued that by using her name without her permission, Out-Kast had defamed her and violated her publicity and trademark rights in their song. Lawyers for OutKast and Arista counter-argued that the song was not false advertising, and had not violated her publicity rights; they also claimed that the First Amendment guaranteed the song protection under the freedom of speech rule. Parks' federal suit was dismissed in 1999, but the U.S. Circuit of Appeals in Cincinnati, Ohio, reinstated some of it, and OutKast's lawyers appealed to the U.S. Supreme Court to block the case from going any further. In December of 2003, Supreme Court justices declined to intervene in the matter, paving the way for the a trial set to begin in January of 2005.

the Atlanta label run by Antonio "L.A." Reid (c. 1958–) that was part of the Arista Records empire. Though they were straightforward rap artists at this early stage in their career, Benjamin and Patton were determined to shake things up. "When I look at the rap videos, it's pretty much the same video over and over," Benjamin explained once to *Newsweek* writer Allison Samuels. "A bunch of women in swimsuits and the guys rapping about money or jewels. Me and Big Boi wanted to change that."

OutKast's first full-length record, *Southernplayalisticadillacmuzik,* was released in 1994, and made it to No. 3 on the Billboard R&B/hip-hop albums chart. They emerged as one of a slew of Atlanta-based groups that were gaining national attention at the time. "Just as Ice Cube had narrated a Westside story and KRS-One told an Eastside version, OutKast … slanged parables" about their hometown, noted *L.A. Weekly* writer Michael Datcher. The pair gained even more listeners in 1996 with *ATLiens,* their follow-up. It featured more of a live-studio sound, favoring real instruments over hi-tech production effects, and had a hit single with "Elevators (Me and You)." It also had a more spaceship-esque mood, which linked them back to Clin-

ton's 1970s-era masterpieces with Parliament-Funkadelic. "When we started doing the more experimental rap, started talking about aliens, that's when more and more white people started coming to the shows," Benjamin told *New York Times* writer Lola Ogunnaike.

In keeping with the New-Age vibe, Benjamin and Patton formed their own boutique label, which they named "Aquemini." The word was made up from a combination of their respective astrological signs, Gemini and Aquarius. They also used it for the title of their third LP. *Aquemini* reached the double-platinum sales mark, thanks in part to the single, "Rosa Parks." Benjamin and Patton began heading in a new direction in the late 1990s, ditching some of the hallmarks of rap style for a more soulful sound. Though both had previously worn baggy jeans and athletic jerseys onstage, Benjamin began sporting far more flamboyant outfits, which included long blond wigs, trousers made of fur, turbans, boas, and checkered-print suits in dazzling colors. He also adopted "André 3000" instead of his longtime "Dre" tag. They remained in partnership with Reid, who took them along when he became president of Arista Records.

## *Stankonia* won rap Grammy

OutKast's major crossover achievement came finally in 2000 with their fourth release, *Stankonia.* The record had a certain psychedelic feel, and produced several hits, among them "Mrs. Jackson," a homage to the grandmother of Benjamin's son with singer Erykah Badu written in the aftermath of a breakup. "I probably would never come out and tell Erykah's mom, 'I'm sorry for what went down,'" he explained about the song's origin in an *Atlanta Journal-Constitution* interview with Craig Seymour. "But music gives you the chance to say what you want to say. And her mom loved it. She's like, 'Where's my publishing check?'"

*Stankonia* also put Atlanta on the musical map for good, with the numerous references to the neighborhoods of East Point and Decatur where they grew up. Critics everywhere wrote enthusiastically of it. It even earned a mention in *Newsweek,* with music writer Lorraine Ali asserting that it "continues OutKast's journey into the weird with a sound that lies somewhere between the jamming madness of Parliament-Funkadelic, the creme de menthe vocals of Al Green and the bumping beats of A Tribe Called Quest."

*Antwan Patton and André Benjamon of OutKast pose in front of the three awards they won at the 2004 Grammy Awards.* AP/Wide World Photos. Reproduced by permission.

*Stankonia* was released in late October of 2000, just after the deadline for releases hoping to be considered for a Grammy Award nomination that year. In early January of 2002, however, it was nominated in five categories, including album of the year. Weeks later, they took home Grammy statues for best rap album of 2001, and best song by a rap duo or group for "Mrs. Jackson."

## Released acclaimed dual CD

Nearly three years went by before OutKast released another studio effort. The long-awaited *Speakerboxxx/The Love Below* made it into stores in late September of 2003, just before the all-important Grammy deadline. It was richly rewarded the following February, winning Grammys for album of the year, best rap album of 2003, and best urban/alternative performance for "Hey Ya!" The dual CD, however, was essentially two separate releases from each OutKast member. Patton's *Speakerboxxx* was a more traditional rap record, and had a hit that made it onto several charts, "The Way You Move."

Andre's *The Love Below* was the funkier record of the two. It originally started out as a soundtrack project that Benjamin began for a film, a love story set in Paris. Though some critics faulted it for mixing too many musical styles, others commended both records for their big-picture vision. "With Speakerboxxx/The Love Below, [Benjamin's] lonely Day-Glo lothario and Big Boi's wise-thug MC have made an LP that offers an outsize artistic vision, not focus-group 'perfection,' as the route to a mass audience," declared *Entertainment Weekly* writer Will Hermes.

The concept-album effort was overshadowed, however, by the massive success of "Hey Ya!" It quickly emerged the biggest hit from *The Love Below,* and became the No. 1 downloaded song on the Internet. Its success boosted the double-album's sales to 3.5 million copies. Much of the rest of Benjamin's effort was reflective. As he explained to a writer for London's *Guardian* newspaper, Alexis Petridis: "In hip-hop, people don't talk about their vulnerable or sensitive side a lot because they're trying to keep it real or be tough— they think it makes them look weak. That's what the Love Below means, that bubbling-under feeling that people don't like to talk about, that dudes try to cover up with machismo."

## No plans for solo careers

Some OutKast fans worried that the dual-album release marked the beginning of the end for the pair, with each too apart musically now to come together again. Both Benjamin and Patton stressed, however, that they were still a team. As Patton explained to Marti Yarbrough in *Jet,* "Both records are OutKast records. They're just from two different perspectives." The former high-school pals worked well together, with Patton overseeing the business side of the partnership from his home in Fayetteville, Georgia. Benjamin, meanwhile, had Hollywood ambitions: he appeared in *Hollywood Homicide* in 2003, and was part of an all-star cast for an adaptation of an Elmore Leonard crime novel, *Be Cool,* released in 2005. Both Benjamin and Patton had also teamed with an Atlanta filmmaker, Bryan Barber, to work on a musical set in a jazz club during the 1920s.

Benjamin and Patton are both fathers. Benjamin's son with Badu, Seven Sirius, divides his time between his parents' homes. Patton has a daughter and two sons. Patton realizes that OutKast's music might reach listeners in unexpected ways, as he told Datcher in the *L.A. Weekly* interview. Once, after a concert, a fan approached him and recounted a story of not "going to class, he just wasn't feeling motivated. He told me he listened to [*Southernplayalisticadillacmuzik*'s] 'Git Up, Git Out' every morning, and that would get him out of the crib so he could go to class," Patton recalled. "He said it helped him graduate from college. That makes me feel good, that we're touching people by just being ourselves and telling our own story."

## For More Information

*Periodicals*

Ali, Lorraine. "So Superfunkyfragelistic! On the Edge with the Weird and Wonderful OutKast." *Newsweek* (October 30, 2000): p. 88.

Arnold, Chuck. "Grammy's Fun Couple: With Six Nominations, Great Beats and Kaleidoscope Clothes, OutKast—The Hottest Act in America—Is Anything But." *People* (February 16, 2004): p. 87.

"Court Gives Rosa Parks the Go-Ahead to Sue Over Rappers' Lyrics.' *Jet* (January 5, 2004): p. 32.

Datcher, Michael. "OutKast's Southern-Fried Hip-Hop Breaks Through." *L.A. Weekly* (December 4, 1998).

Hermes, Will. "Fully Funktional: OutKast Propel Hip-Hop to New Heights with Their Madly Ambitious, Soul-Sparking Solo CDs." *Entertainment Weekly* (September 19, 2003): p. 83.

Lester, Paul. "Friday Review." *Guardian* (London, England) (May 18, 2001): p. 6.

Ogunnaike, Lola. "Outkast, Rap's Odd Couple: Gangsta Meets Granola." *New York Times* (September 7, 2003): p. AR87.

Petridis, Alexis. "The Friday Interview." *Guardian* (London, England) (November 7, 2003): p. 8.

Samuels, Allison. "Twins Beneath The Skin: The Two Guys Who Make up the Quirky Hip-Hop Unit Outkast Couldn't Be More Different—And on Their New Album, Each One Gets His Own Disc. Can This Marriage Be Saved?" *Newsweek* (September 22, 2003): p. 86.

Seymour, Craig. "Steps to Success." *Atlanta Journal-Constitution* (February 26, 2002): p. E1.

"Southern-Fried Hip-Hop: Down-Home Lyrics and Strong Dance Grooves Are Ingredients of a Tasty Menu." *Ebony* (January 2004): p. 74.

Tyrangiel, Josh. "Dysfunktion Junction: OutKast, the Planet's Best Rap Duo, Is One Odd Couple." *Time* (September 29, 2003): p. 71.

Yarbrough, Marti. "OutKast: Music's Favorite Odd Couple Breaks the Hip-Hop Mold." *Jet* (February 2, 2004): p. 58

# Larry Page and Sergey Brin

## Larry Page

*c. 1973* • *East Lansing, Michigan*

Entrepreneur

## Sergey Brin

*August 21, 1973* • *Moscow, Russia*

Entrepreneur

Larry Page and Sergey Brin founded Google, the Internet search engine, while they were graduate students at Stanford University in Palo Alto, California. Since its founding in 1998, Google has become one of the most successful dot-com businesses in history. Both Page and Brin were reluctant entrepreneurs who were committed to developing their company on their own terms, not those dictated by the prevailing business culture.

### Not instant best friends

Page grew up in the East Lansing, Michigan, area, where his father, Carl Victor Page, was a professor of computer science at Michigan State University. The senior Page was also an early pioneer in the field of artificial intelligence, and reportedly gave his young son his first computer when Larry was just six years old. Several years later Page entered the University of Michigan, where he earned an undergraduate degree in engineering with a concentration in computer engineering.

*Larry Page (left) and Sergey Brin.*
AP/Wide World Photos. Reproduced by permission.

His first jobs were at Advanced Management Systems in Washington, D.C., and then at a company called CogniTek in Evanston, Illinois.

An innovative thinker with a sense of humor as well, Page once built a working ink-jet printer out of Lego blocks. He was eager to advance in his career, and decided to study for a Ph.D degree. He was admitted to the prestigious doctoral program in computer science at Stanford University. On an introductory weekend at the Palo Alto campus that had been arranged for new students, he met Sergey Brin. A native of Moscow, Russia, Brin was also the son of a professor, and came to the United States with his family when he was six. His father taught math at the University of Maryland, and it was from that school's College Park campus that Brin earned an undergraduate degree in computer science and math.

Brin was already enrolled in Stanford's PhD program when Page arrived in 1995. As Brin explained to Robert McGarvey of *Technology Review,* "I was working on data mining, the idea of taking large amounts of data, analyzing it for patterns and trying to extract relationships that are useful." One weekend Brin was assigned to a team that showed the new doctoral students around campus, and Page was in his group. Industry lore claims they argued the whole time, but soon found themselves working together on a research project. That 1996 paper, "Anatomy of a Large-Scale Hypertextual Web Search Engine," became the basis for the Google search engine.

## A hit with fellow students

Page and Brin created an algorithm, or set of step-by-step instructions for solving a specific computer task. Their algorithm searched all the hypertext documents in cyberspace, which are the basis for Web pages on the Internet. A typical search engine such as Hot Bot, which was popular at one time in the mid-1990s, worked by looking for a term the user entered—"New York Yankees," for example—in all of those documents. If the phrase "New York Yankees" was written into one Web site's hypertext code several dozen or even a hundred times, that document would come up first in the search results. But it might just turn out to be an Internet store that sold sports memorabilia.

> **"I hope they will be able to return answers, not just documents.... In the future, Google will be your interface to all the world's knowledge—not just web pages."**
>
> **Sergey Brin, *Guardian* (London, England), November 23, 2000.**

Page and Brin wanted to create a search tool that would find the most relevant Web page first. If someone typed in "New York Yankees," for example, the official Yankees site would be the first result returned. Their algorithm analyzed the "back links" in a hypertext document, or how many times other sites linked to it—the more links, the higher the relevancy of the page. As an article in *Time* explained, their search technology was the first to "treat the Internet as a democracy. Google interprets connections between websites as votes. The most linked-to sites win on the Google usefulness ballot and rise to the top of the search results."

The search engine with Page and Brin's unique algorithm was initially named "Backrub," but they later settled on "PageRank," named after Page. It soon caught on with other Stanford users when Page and Brin let them try it out. The two set up a simple search page for users, because they did not have a web page developer to create anything very

## Google Pranks

The freewheeling corporate culture at Google has produced the occasional prank since its founding. The company had been known to post fake press releases around April 1, or April Fools' Day. In 2000, for example, it launched "MentalPlex," which offered Google site visitors the ability to "search smarter and faster" by peering into a circle with shifting colors.

In 2003 Google explained its novel search technology "PigeonRank" in an April Fools' Day insertion on their Web site that offered a behind-the-scenes glimpse into "the technology behind Google's great results." It was pigeons, the page explained, that helped deliver such quick and accurate search results. In a FAQ, or Frequently Asked Questions, section of the page, it addressed the question, "Aren't pigeons really stupid? How do they do this?" Google responded, "While no pigeon has actually been confirmed for a seat on the Supreme Court, pigeons are surprisingly adept at making instant judgments when confronted with difficult choices."

impressive. They also began stringing together the necessary computing power to handle searches by multiple users, by using any computer part they could find. As their search engine grew in popularity among Stanford users, it needed more and more servers to process the queries. "At Stanford we'd stand on the loading dock and try to snag computers as they came in," Page recalled to McGarvey. "We would see who got 20 computers and ask them if they could spare one."

## Maxed out credit cards

During this time Page and Brin were running the project out of their dorm rooms at Stanford. Page's room served as the data hub, while Brin's was the business office. But they were reluctant entrepreneurs, not wanting to shelve their Ph.D. studies and join the dot-com rush of the era. In mid-1998 they finally relented. "Pretty soon, we had 10,000 searches a day," Page told *Newsweek*'s Steven Levy. "And we figured, maybe this is really real." They initially set out just to defray their costs. "We spent about $15,000 on a terabyte [one million megabytes] of disks," Brin explained to McGarvey. "We spread that across three credit cards. Once we did that, we wrote up a business plan."

Page and Brin had the idea to license their PageRank technology to other companies to pay off their credit card debt, but none were interested. David Filo (1966–), another Stanford graduate who had started Yahoo.com, suggested they form a search-engine company. They named their company "Google," after the mathematical term Googol, which specified the number one followed by a hundred zeros. They took it to Andy Bechtolsheim (1956–), a Stanford graduate and co-founder of Sun Microsystems. One of their professors set up an in an early morning meeting with Bechtolsheim. They showed him their Google demo, but Bechtolsheim had another meeting on his schedule that morning, and needed to leave. He liked their idea, however, and offered to write them a check on the spot for seed money. It was for $100,000, and was made out to "Google." In order to deposit it, Page and Brin first needed to open a bank account with their company name on it.

Page and Brin went on to raise more money from friends, family, and then from venture capital firms that funded new businesses. By the end of 1999 they had set up headquarters in an office park in Mountain View, and had officially launched the site. In June of 2000, Google reached an important hallmark: it had indexed one billion Internet URLs, or Uniform Resource Locators. A URL is the World Wide Web address of a site on the Internet. Reaching the one-billion mark made Google the most comprehensive search engine on the Web.

## Hired industry pro

In their first years in business, Brin served as president, while Page was the chief executive officer. The company continued to grow exponentially during 2001. Google even became a verb—to "Google" someone or something meant to search for it via the engine, but it was most commonly used in reference to checking out the Web presence of potential dates. Page and Brin's company was the subject of articles in mainstream publications, but they continually rejected offers to go public—make their company a publicly traded one on Wall Street. They did, however, hire Eric Schmidt (1955–) as chief executive officer and board chair in 2001. Schmidt was a veteran of Sun, where he had served as chief technology officer. As Brin explained to Betsy Cummings in *Sales & Marketing Management,* "Larry and I have done a good job," but conceded that "the probability of doing something dumb" was still likely. "It's clear we need some international strategy, and Eric brings that."

Google kept expanding in cyberspace. It added search capabilities in dozens of languages, and began partnering with overseas sites as well. It also attracted legions of devoted new employees. Its headquarters were informally known as the "Googleplex," and workers were relatively free to make their own hours, with the idea that employees should be able to work when they felt they were most productive. Google staff were also encouraged to use 80 percent of their work hours on regular work, and the other 20 percent on projects of their own design. One of those side projects emerged as Orkut.com, a harder-to-join version of the social-networking phenomenon Friendster.com. Orkut was named after the Google engineer who created it, Orkut Buyukkokten.

*The homepage for the Google News web site.* © James Leynse/Corbis.

Page and Brin strove to keep Google's corporate culture relaxed in other ways, which they felt benefited the company in the long run. Its perks were legendary. There was free Ben and Jerry's ice cream, an on-site masseuse, a ping-pong table, yoga classes, and even a staff physician. Employees could bring their dogs to work, and the company cafeteria was run by a professional chef who used to work for the rock band the Grateful Dead. Brin discussed his management philosophy with Cummings. "Since we started the company, we've grown twenty percent per month. Our employees can do whatever they want."

## Long-awaited IPO

By early 2004 Google was one of the most-visited Web sites in the world. Its servers handled some 138,000 search queries per minute, or about two hundred million daily. Analysts believed it was taking in approximately $1 billion in revenues annually, and the company finally announced plans to become a publicly traded company with an initial public offering (IPO) of stock. Theirs, however, would utilize a unique online auction process to sell its first shares to the public. This meant that the large Wall Street firms that handled the IPO underwriting—which investigated the company's books and then placed a monetary value on it—would not be able to give the first shares out to their top clients as a perk. It was estimated that Google was going to be valued at least at $15 billion, and possibly even as high as $30 billion.

Page and Brin each own thirty-eight million shares of Google stock. They would become overnight millionaires when Google began trading on the NASDAQ, or National Association of Securities Dealers Automatic Quotation system, sometime in 2004. Business journalists were calling it the most hotly anticipated IPO of the post-dot-com era. Many other Internet companies had quickly become publicly traded ones in the late 1990s, but began to crash when the economy slowed over the next few years. Just prior to launching their IPO, Google entered a legally required "quiet period," in which they were not allowed to discuss their plans or strategies with the press. Brin told Levy in *Newsweek* just before that period that he and Page were content to keep tinkering with their research-paper idea. "I think we're pretty far along compared to 10 years ago," he said. "At the same time, where can you go? Certainly if you had all the world's information directly attached to your brain, or an artificial brain that was smarter than your brain, you'd be better off. Between that and today, there's plenty of space to cover."

## For More Information

### *Periodicals*

Cummings, Betsy. "Beating the Odds: Now That Frivolity Has Killed Many a Start-Up, Relaxed Management, On-Site Restaurants, and In-House Massages Seem Like Dot-Com Death Wishes. Google.com Proves Otherwise—Thanks to Top-Rate Technology, a Rare Sales Model, and an Aggressive Vision for What's Ahead." *Sales & Marketing Management* (March 2002): p. 24.

Flynn, Laurie J. "2 Wild and Crazy Guys (Soon to Be Billionaires), and Hoping to Keep It That Way." *New York Times* (April 30, 2004): p. C6.

Helmore, Edward. "Float Revolution: Google Takes the High Road: The Founders of the Internet Phenomenon Have Announced Flotation Plans — But They Are Determined to Go Public in Their Own Inimitable Fashion." *Observer* (London, England) (May 2, 2004): p. 3.

"In Search of Google: Watch out, Yahoo. There's a Search Engine Out There with Uncanny Speed and Accuracy. And It's Way Cool." *Time* (August 21, 2000): p. 66.

Keegan, Victor. "Online: Working It Out: Searching Questions: Sergey Brin Is the President and Co-Founder of the Search Engine Google, Which Was Set Up in 1998." *Guardian* (London, England) (November 23, 2000): p. 4.

Levy, Steven. "All Eyes on Google; In Six Short Years, Two Stanford Grad Students Turned a Simple Idea into a Multibillion-Dollar Phenomenon and Changed Our Lives. Now Competitors Are Searching for a Way to Dethrone the Latest Princes of the Net." *Newsweek* (March 29, 2004): p. 48.

Levy, Steven. "The World According to Google: What If You Had a Magic Tool That Let You Find Out Almost Anything in Less than a Second? Millions of People Already Have It—and It's Changing the Way We Live." *Newsweek* (December 16, 2002): p. 46.

McGarvey, Robert. "Search Us, Says Google." *Technology Review* (November 2000): p. 108.

Poliski, Iris. "Page Revs up Google's Engine: The Google Search Engine is Virtually a Household Name among Computer Users, and Larry Page, Its Developer, Was Voted R&D's Innovator of the Year for Bringing It to Fruition. Not Only Is Google a Powerful Finder, Its Spinoffs May Change Computing History." *R & D* (November 2002): p. 40.

Sappenfield, Mark. "A Culture of Idealists Creates Startup Success Google Founders Hold Firm to Their Geeky Roots." *Seattle Times* (April 30, 2004): p. E4.

Waters, Richard. "Idealists Bound for Reality: Men in the News Sergey Brin and Larry Page: As Google Prepares For Its Stock Market Debut, Richard Waters Asks How the Men Who Founded the World's Most Popular Search Engine Will Cope with the Transition from Internet Visionaries to Corporate Billionaires." *Financial Times* (October 25, 2003): p. 15.

### Web Sites

"The Google Timeline." *Google.com.* http://www.google.com/corporate/ timeline.html (accessed on July 13, 2004).

"Our Search: Google Technology." *Google.com.* http://www.google.com/ technology/pigeonrank.html (accessed on July 13, 2004).

# Christopher Paolini

Photograph by Denay Wilding.

*1984*

Author

**A**uthor Christopher Paolini not only writes about fantasy, he lives it. When he was a mere fifteen years old, he penned a sweeping epic called *Eragon,* which was eventually discovered by a New York publisher—and by thousands of readers. In 2003 the book nestled comfortably on bestseller lists, and by 2004 a movie based on the magnificent tale of a boy and a brilliant blue dragon was poised to take flight. Paolini was also hard at work writing the second and third installments in the Inheritance trilogy. In a *teenreads.com* interview, the author and boy wonder promised fans that future books would include the same "breathtaking locations, thrilling battles, and searching introspection as Eragon—in addition to true love."

## A reluctant reader

In 1984, when Christopher Paolini was born, his mother, Talita, quit her job as a Montessori preschool teacher to devote her time to raising her new son. Montessori is a system of learning developed by Italian educator Maria Montessori (1870–1952); some of its features include a focus on individual instruction and an early development of writing skills. Talita used the Montessori method to teach Christopher at home, and two years later when sister Angela came along, she, too, became part of the Paolini classroom. Since some of the materials in a Montessori school are expensive, Talita experimented and came up with creative alternatives to inspire and educate her children. She was so successful that by the time Christopher, and later Angela, turned three years old, they were both comfortably working at a first-grade level.

"I enjoy fantasy because it allows me to visit lands that have never existed, to see things that never could exist, to experience daring adventures with interesting characters, and most importantly, to feel the sense of magic in the world."

When Christopher was old enough to attend public school, his parents were worried that he would be bored by a traditional curriculum, so they thought long and hard and decided to educate him at home. In fact, focusing on their children was such a top priority that the Paolinis made a deliberate choice to live simply, drawing small salaries from Kenneth Paolini's home-based publishing company. In interviews Paolini has talked about the nurturing environment his parents created for him, and he credits them for being his inspiration. He has also admitted that he was not always a receptive student. A particularly interesting note is that Paolini was a reluctant reader. When he was about three or four, he refused to learn to read, but his mother worked patiently with him until one day a door opened that would change his life.

That door was his first visit to the library. In his essay titled "Dragon Tales," Paolini described going to the library with his mother and being attracted to a series of mystery books with colorful spines. He

## The Wonderful World of Teen Authors

**C**hristopher Paolini was indeed a boy wonder, writing his first book at age fifteen, but American publishing is filled with stories written by young authors. Some have been published quite recently, while others go back a number of years. The following is just a short list of teen writers; the age listed indicates how old the author was when he or she wrote their first work.

Amelia Atwater-Rhodes (14 years old): *In the Forests of the Night* (1999); *Demon in My View* (2000); *Shattered Mirror* (2001); *Midnight Predator* (2002); *Hawksong* (2003); *Snakecharm* (2004).

Walter Farley (15 years old): *The Black Stallion* (although the book was published in 1941, Farley wrote the first draft of *Stallion* while still a student at Erasmus High School in New York City).

Miles Franklin (16 years old): *My Brilliant Career* (1901).

Kimberly Fuller (16 years old): *Home* (1997).

S. E. Hinton (16 years old): *Outsiders* (1967); *That was Then, This is Now* (1971); *Rumble Fish* (1975); *Tex* (1979); *Taming the Star Runner* (1988); *Hawks Harbor* (2004).

Gordan Korman (14 years old): Korman is a prolific writer who began his popular Macdonald Hall series with *This Can't Be Happening at Macdonald Hall* (1977).

Benjamin Lebert (16 years old): *Crazy* (2000; first American translation from the German).

Megan McNeil Libby (16 years old): *Postcards from France* (1998).

Dav Pilkey (19 years old): *World War Won* (1987); Pilkey went on to achieve fame as the author of the well-known Captain Underpants series.

Trope, Zoe (15 years old): *Please Don't Kill the Freshman: A Memoir* (c. 2003).

took one home and, according to Paolini, something clicked. He was spellbound by the characters, the dialogue, and the fascinating situations. "From then on," wrote Paolini, "I've been in love with the written word." He went on to devour books of all kinds—classics, myths, thrillers, science fiction, anything that seemed interesting. In particular, he was drawn to the fantasy genre and to writers who wrote tales about heroes and elves, swordfights and quests and, especially, dragons.

## A writer of dragons

Paolini often found himself daydreaming about dragons when he was riding in the car, when he was taking a shower, when he was supposed to be doing his homework. While he was growing up he captured some of his daydreams on paper, writing poems and short stories that featured dragons and were set in magical places. Paolini did not take a real stab at writing a longer piece until he graduated from high school in 1999, at the age of fifteen. According to Paolini, he did not set out to get published; instead, he viewed writing a book-length work as a kind of personal challenge.

Paolini had ideas swimming around in his head, but he realized that he knew very little about the actual art of writing—for example, how to construct a plot line. So he set out to do some research. He studied several books on writing, including *Characters and Viewpoint* (1988) by Orson Scott Card and Robert McKee's *Story* (1997), which helped him to sketch out a nine-page summary. Paolini then spent the next year fleshing out his story, writing sporadically at first, but then picking up the pace. The task went much more quickly after he learned how to type.

As Paolini explained in "Dragon Tales," he tried to imbue his story with the same elements he found most compelling in books: "an intelligent hero; lavish descriptions; exotic locations; dragons; elves; dwarves; magic; and above all else, a sense of awe and wonder." In particular, he drew upon the works of some of his favorite fantasy authors for inspiration, including J. R. R. Tolkien (1892–1973), author of The Lord of the Rings trilogy, and Anne McCaffrey (1926–), an American writer famous for her Dragonriders of Pern series. The result was a book called *Eragon.*

*Eragon* follows the adventures of a fifteen-year-old farm boy who finds a mysterious gemstone covered with white veins. It is actually a dragon's egg, and when the egg hatches and a magnificent blue dragon emerges, the boy's life is changed forever. Eragon names the dragon Saphira, and the two become so inseparable that they share their innermost thoughts and feelings. Their bond is challenged, however, by an evil tyrant named King Galbatorix. A hundred years earlier, Galbatorix had outlawed dragons and destroyed the Dragon Riders, the lodge of dragon-riding warriors who protected them. When the king becomes aware that Eragon is the first of a new generation of Dragon Riders, he has his family killed and plots to capture the boy and his blue-scaled companion. Eragon and Saphira embark on a journey of escape and revenge, and along the way meet up with a wise magician, elves, dwarves, and several beautiful maidens.

## Polishing up his prose

Paolini spent the bulk of 2000 reworking his first draft, smoothing out problems and fine-tuning such things as language and landscape. The young author introduces no less than three languages in *Eragon*: the elves speak a language based on Old Norse (the languages of medieval Scandinavia), which Paolini spent months studying; and the dwarves and Urgals (the fanged army of King Galbarotix) each speak a language made up entirely by Paolini. To help readers along, Paolini created a glossary that appears at the end of the finished book.

For the mythical setting of Alagaësia, Paolini turned to the natural landscape of his own home state. The Paolinis live in Livingston, Montana, located in the scenic Paradise Valley just north of Yellowstone Park. Years of hiking through such rugged and beautiful terrain helped Paolini create a vivid world that is both fantastic and true-to-life. For example, the Beor Mountains that are featured in *Eragon* are an exaggerated version of the Beartooth Mountains of Montana.

By 2001 Paolini had a second draft, but he was still not satisfied, so he turned the book over to his parents for editing. They helped him streamline some of the plot sequences, clarify some of the concepts, and pare back some of what Paolini called "the bloat." Kenneth and Talita Paolini were so impressed by the finished product, and believed in the manuscript so much, that they decided to throw themselves into publishing it. Instead of going the traditional route and shopping the book around to established publishing houses, they decided to publish it themselves. As Paolini told teenreads.com, "We wanted to retain financial and creative control over the book. Also, we were excited by the prospect of working on this project as a family." Kenneth formatted the book on his computer, and the young Paolini, who is also a budding artist, drew the maps to accompany the text. He designed the book's front cover and produced a self-portrait to grace the back cover.

## The fantasy comes true

In 2002 the Paolinis had *Eragon* published privately, and with ten thousand copies in hand, they set out to promote the book for the rest of the year. Paolini and his mother became the marketing masterminds, but the entire family traveled across the country, stopping at bookstores, schools, libraries, and fairs. Paolini even decided to forego college to promote his book. He had previously been accepted to Reed College in Portland, Oregon. In an interview with Kit Spring of *The UK Guardian Unlimited,* Paolini described the book's promotion as a stressful experience. The young author gave presentations dressed as a medieval storyteller, and he found himself spending entire days talking ceaselessly about his book.

The nonstop tour was exhausting, but Paolini also felt the added pressure of becoming his family's breadwinner. As he explained to Spring, "Selling the book meant putting food on the table." Sales were going well, but not well enough, and by the end of 2002, the Paolinis were afraid that they might have to

*Christopher Paolini reads during a book signing at Borders in Birmingham, MI.* Photograph by Denay Wilding.

sell their home to make ends meet. Just when things looked bleak, providence stepped in by way of a famous fan. Author Carl Hiaasen (1953–) and his family were on vacation in Montana, and when they stopped at a local bookstore, Hiaasen's stepson picked up a copy of *Eragon.* He loved it so much that he showed it to Hiaasen, who promptly sent the book to his editor at Alfred A. Knopf Publishers in New York City.

Knopf purchased the book for an undisclosed six-figure sum, along with the rights to the next two books in the trilogy. Paolini had always envisioned *Eragon* as the first in a series of three books. When the book was released in August of 2003, it debuted at number three on the *New York Times* children's bestseller list, and Paolini was off on another whirlwind round of promotions. This time, however, things were a bit different, since he was appearing on such high-profile television programs as the *Today Show,* and being interviewed by national magazines including *People Weekly, Newsweek,* and *Time.* In 2004, Paolini extended his tour to Great Britain.

*Eragon* was also making the rounds of critics, who gave the book mixed reviews. Some focused on flaws and weaknesses, claiming that the book was a novelty and that its success was actually the result of the author's young age. Others pointed out faults, but still felt that *Eragon* was an appealing fantasy novel that showed great promise. For example, Liz Rosenberg of the *New York Times Book Review* claimed that the "plot stumbles and jerks along, with gaps in logic." But she also admitted that "for all its flaws, [the book] is an authentic work of great talent."

## Future flights of fiction

Fans agreed with Rosenberg's final pronouncement, and *Eragon* quickly developed a cult following. In mid-2004 it remained at the top of the *New York Times* bestseller list, flip-flopping between the number one and the number two spots, vying for the top spot with *Harry Potter and the Order of the Phoenix,* by popular British author J. K. Rowling (c. 1966–). The privately published editions of *Eragon* became hot collectors' items, bringing up to $1,000 per copy. Even the first Knopf edition became sought after, selling for close to $300.

Throughout his many interviews, Paolini seemed thrilled by all the attention, but the slightly built, bespectacled young man still kept his feet firmly planted on the ground. After all, he had to stay focused because he had two books in the wings: *Eldest,* which was expected to be released in August of 2005, and *Empire,* slated to be published in the fall of 2006. In the meantime, Paolini was also hard at work writing the screenplay for *Eragon,* tentatively scheduled to hit theaters in time for Christmas of 2005.

Although the pressure was on to perform, the financial pressure was lightened and the Paolinis were living comfortably. Again, Christopher Paolini kept things in perspective. He claimed that he has allowed himself one extravagance, a replica Viking sword, which he carries with him around the house. He told *Book Browse,* "There's no guarantee it will last…. Readers have fallen in love with [Eragon], thousands of people are reading it. I can't really ask for more."

## For More Information

### Books
Paolini, Christopher. *Eragon.* New York: Alfred A. Knopf, 2003.

### Periodicals
Paolini, Christopher. "How I Write: Interview with Christopher Paolini." *Writer* (March 2004): p. 66.

Rosenberg, Liz. Review of *Eragon. New York Times Book Review* (November 16, 2003): p. 58.

### Web Sites
"Author Profile: Christopher Paolini." *teenreads.com* (September 2003). http://www.teenreads.com/authors/au-paolini-christopher.asp (accessed on July 12, 2004).

"Christopher Paolini: Biography and Interview." *Bookbrowse.com* (September 2003). http://www.bookbrowse.com/index.cfm?page=author&authorID=934 (accessed on July 12, 2004).

*Eragon.* http://www.randomhouse.com/teens/eragon (accessed on July 12, 2004).

Paolini, Christopher. "Dragon Tales: An Essay on Becoming a Writer." *Eragon.* http://www.randomhouse.com/teens/eragon/dragontales.htm (accessed on July 12, 2004).

Spring, Kit. "Elf and Efficiency." *UK Guardian Unlimited* (January 25, 2004). http://books.guardian.co.uk/departments/childrenandteens/story/0,6000,1130351,00.html (accessed on July 12, 2004).

Weich, David. "Author Interviews: Philip Pullman, Tamora Pierce, and Christopher Paolini Talk Fantasy Fiction." *Powells.com* (June 31, 2003). http://www.powells.com/authors/paolini.html (accessed on July 12, 2004).

# Linda Sue Park

Clarion Books.

**March 25, 1960** · **Urbana, Illinois**

## Author

Linda Sue Park began writing when she was in kindergarten, and became a professional writer when she published her first poem at age nine. She went on to become a journalist, a food critic, and an English teacher, but Park did not test her hand at writing fiction until she was in her mid-thirties, at the same time that she began to explore her Korean heritage in earnest. Her research resulted in a treasure trove of children's books, each of which delves into a different piece of Korean history. In 2002 Park was awarded the Newbery Medal for her third novel, *A Single Shard,* which follows the adventures of a twelfth-century orphan named Tree-ear. The Newbery is awarded by the American Library Association, and is given to the most distinguished American children's book published in the previous year. Park became the first Korean American to take home the honor.

### A maniacal reader

Linda Sue Park was born on March 25, 1960, in Urbana, Illinois, the

U·X·L newsmakers · *volume 3*

daughter of Eung Won Ed, a computer analyst, and Susie Kim, a teacher. Her parents were Korean immigrants who moved to the United States in the 1950s; they were among the first wave of Koreans to migrate to America following World War II (1939–45). Once in the United States, the Parks did their best to assimilate to their adopted country and leave the past behind. As a result, Linda Sue grew up knowing very little about her family's background. As she explained in a *Time for Kids* interview, "My parents thought the best way to help us succeed was to become very American, which meant only speaking English at home. We celebrated certain holidays and upheld a few traditions, but I don't actually speak Korean."

## "One of the best things about writing is that it makes you a better observer—pay attention to people and things because you never know what might inspire a story."

One way that Park was introduced to American culture was through books. In several interviews, she fondly remembered her father taking her to the library every two weeks beginning when she was very young. Because of those visits, Park became what she called a "maniacal reader." "It was by far my favorite activity," she told Cynthia Leitich Smith in an interview. Park read everything from Nancy Drew mysteries to award-winning children's books, and "everything in between." She also described herself as a re-reader, someone who comes back to old favorites again and again. Some of her all-time favorite writers were Laura Ingalls Wilder (1867–1957), author of the *Little House* series, and award-winning contemporary author E. L. Konigsburg (1930–).

Reading was not Park's only passion; she also loved to write. She began to scribble stories and poems when she was still in kindergarten, and when she was just nine years old she had her first poem published in a magazine called *Trailblazer*. The poem was a haiku, a form of Japanese nature poetry that is unrhymed and composed of

## Korean Kite Fighting

In Korean history, kite flying can be traced back to 637 C.E., during the first year of the reign of Queen Chindok of Silla, when a Korean general named Kim Yu-Sin used a kite to subdue a revolt. His army refused to follow his lead because they had seen a shooting star, which they believed to be a bad omen. To rally his troops, the general launched a kite carrying a burning ball; the superstitious soldiers thought the star (or bad omen) was returning to heaven, so they joined in the fight and defeated the rebels. Over time, kites were used for various military purposes, but eventually kite flying became a popular sport among Koreans both young and old. To this day, kite festivals are especially popular around holidays such as the Lunar New Year.

Kite festivals gave birth to kite fighting. The purpose of a kite-fighting competition is to bring down all other kites—the last one remaining is the winner. A fighter kite is usually small and rectangular in shape. It looks quite simple in design, but it is actually very tough. The most popular type of kite, called a shield kite, is made from five bamboo sticks and covered with traditional Korean mulberry paper. Such combat kites are tail-less; it is the kite string that is the most important component since it is the key to a competitor's attack strategy. The silken string is reinforced with a layer of adhesive, such as rice glue or varnish. It is then coated with glass powder, ground pottery, or even knife blades—anything sharp enough for a flyer to cut his opponent's line and bring down his kite.

three lines containing a certain number of syllables: the first line has five syllables, the second has seven, and the third has five. Park was paid one dollar for her poem, which she gave to her father as a Christmas present. He framed the check, which still hangs over his office desk. Park continued to be published in magazines for children throughout elementary and high school.

Park has claimed that she never consciously set out to become a professional writer, but she does admit that every decision she made revolved around her love of reading and writing. After graduating from high school she headed to Stanford University in Palo Alto, California, where she majored in English. "I majored in English," Park told Smith, "so I could read and write all the time." Not all of her time, however, was spent pouring over books. Park also participated in sports, and was an accomplished gymnast.

## Children's author in the making

In 1981 the aspiring author graduated from Stanford and took a job as a public relations writer for Amoco Oil Company. It was not exactly the kind of writing she had in mind, but it did give Park her first taste of professional life. While working at Amoco, she also met her future husband, a journalist from Ireland named Ben Dobbin. In 1983, when Dobbin returned to Ireland, Park decided to go with him. The two lived in Dublin, where Park studied literature at Trinity College. Park and Dobbin married in 1984 and moved to London, where Park attended Birkbeck College, earning a master's degree in 1988. The London years were busy ones. In addition to taking classes, Park had two children, Anna and Sean. She also taught English as a Second Language to college students, and tried her hand at a number of writing jobs. At various times Park worked as a copywriter at an advertising company and as a writer of restaurant reviews. And, of course, she continued to write poetry.

In 1990 Park and her family moved back to the United States because of Dobbin's job. She taught English, and her poems were regularly published in small reviews. By the mid-1990s, however, she began to experiment with longer works of fiction. Park had dabbled in fiction before, but a turning point took place when she started to do some real research into Korean history. She was partly motivated to explore her roots because of her children, since she wanted to make sure they would have a chance to connect with both their Irish and Korean grandparents. It was also a personal journey. As Park explained to Cecelia Goodnow of the *Seattle Post-Intelligencer,* "It definitely was a personal sort of search for me." Park interviewed family members, and also dipped into her own memories, which included a visit to Korea that took place when she was eleven years old. Park was particularly inspired by a collection of Korean folktales that she had read as a child, called *Tales of a Korean Grandmother* by Frances Carpenter.

Park began by writing short stories based on these Korean folktales, but an original story was taking shape in her head. She did not know whether it was meant to be a picture book or a short story, or something much longer. Several thousand words later it became evident that she was producing a novel-length book for children. That book would eventually become her first published work of fiction, *Seesaw Girl.* Writing a book for children seemed to come naturally to Park. After all, she had spent so much of her life reading children's books that, as she commented to Cynthia Leitich Smith, "the structure of those books got sort of 'hard-wired' into my brain." Park also felt that her years of writing poetry served as the perfect training ground for writing for children. "Children's books and poetry have a nice merging point which is no fat," she explained in an interview with the *Alsop Review.* "You can't write a lazy line or a line with too many words."

Writing may have come easily to her, but publishing a manuscript did not. Without an agent or any connections in the publishing industry, Park initially sent her work out willy-nilly. As she told Smith, she "did absolutely everything wrong." By the time she finished her first long manuscript, however, Park had learned how to approach publishers in a professional manner. She submitted sample chapters of *Seesaw Girl* to six publishing houses; all six asked to see a complete manuscript. The book was eventually published by Clarion Books in 1997.

## Seesaws and kites

*Seesaw Girl* is the story of Jade Blossom, a twelve-year-old girl growing up in an aristocratic household in seventeenth-century Korea. The custom of the times forbade young girls of social standing from leaving their family compounds until they were married. As a result, Jade is curious about the world outside, especially when Willow, her best friend and aunt, marries and leaves her behind. Jade arranges a day of escape, but what she encounters is not all beautiful, and she realizes that her family home provides not so much imprisonment as protection. When she returns to her family, she understands she must be content with catching glimpses of the world thanks to a stand-up seesaw built close to the compound walls. Critics especially praised Park for her faithful depiction of daily life in seventeenth-century Korea. As Barbara Scotto of *School Library Journal* commented, "Like Jade's stand-up seesaw, Park's novel offers readers a brief but enticing glimpse at another time and place."

Park drew upon family experiences to flesh out aspects of *Seesaw Girl*. When Park was young, for example, her mother built a Korean seesaw for Park and her brother in their backyard. A Korean seesaw is similar to an American seesaw in that a plank of wood is balanced across a central point; the difference is that players stand on each end (instead of sitting) and jump. "It takes some practice," Park explained to Julie Durango on By the Book Web site in 2000. "The timing is quite precise—the 'jumper' has to take off at the exact moment that the 'flyer' lands."

In her next book, *The Kite Fighters* (2000), Park again turned to family stories for inspiration, this time creating a work that would be a tribute to her father. At the center of the story is the rivalry between two kite-flying brothers, Kee-sup and Young-sup, who live in Seoul, Korea, in 1473. Kite fighting was a popular sport in the late fifteenth century, and each brother has his own unique talent. Older brother Kee-sup is gifted at kite design and construction, while Young-sup is a masterful kite flyer who has the ability to make kites dance in the wind. When the boy-king of Korea learns of their skills he enlists the boys to create a perfect kite for the all-important New Year's competition. In the book Park not only described the intricate world of kite fighting, but also explored the traditional roles the boys played, based on their position in the family.

Park researched the art of kite design and the sport of kite fighting, but she especially relied on her father's expertise, since he had been a devoted kite flyer as a boy. After the manuscript was finished, Eung Won read over the text to make sure the descriptions were accurate; he also served as the book's illustrator, contributing the decorations that open each chapter. In addition, Park's father offered insight into his experience as a second son in a traditional Korean household. Reviewers paid particular attention to the fact that although Park's story takes place in medieval Korea, her characters face many of the problems siblings face today. The author was quick to point out, however, that historical accuracy is important. As she explained to *Writer's Digest,* "I want readers to be able to relate to the characters, but at the same time I want the characters to be grounded in their place and time."

## Newbery winner

Park spends many hours on the Internet and at the library doing research for her books, and along the way she tucks away notes and idea for future stories. Back in 1996, while investigating the background for *Seesaw Girl,* she came across references to celadon, a type of pottery introduced in Korea that is considered to be among the finest in the world. "I liked that," Park commented to *Writer's Digest,* "the idea of a little tiny country being the best at something." As a result, in

2001, celadon pottery formed the basis of her award-winning book *A Single Shard,* which, like her previous works, takes place in early Korea. This time the action is set in the twelfth century and follows the adventures of an orphaned boy named Tree-ear, who becomes an apprentice to Min, a master potter in his village of Ch'ulp'o.

In an interview with *Alsop Review,* Park called *A Single Shard* her "once in a lifetime 'muse' experience," explaining that the book just poured out of her, page after page. Readers and reviewers agreed that *Shard* was indeed magical, and in 2002 Park was awarded the Newbery Medal, one of the highest honors in the nation for a children's book. She spent the better part of the next year traveling around the country, appearing at book signings and giving readings. She also became quite famous in Korea, making headline news and receiving congratulations from Korean well-wishers. The experience was all very "thrilling and humbling," Park told Durango. She had little time, however, to rest on her laurels, since Park was busy putting the finishing touches on her next book, which many claim is her most powerful yet, perhaps because it was a labor of love.

*When My Name was Keoko,* published in 2002, is based on her parents' memories of growing up in Korea during the Japanese occupation of their country. After taking control of Korea in 1910, the Japanese government attempted to erase Korean traditions and customs, going so far as to make Koreans take Japanese names. "Keoko was my mother's Japanese name," Park explained in the *Time for Kids* interview. "That's where the title comes from." When Park was a young girl, her parents did not talk about their painful experiences, but after she began her research they opened up. "I asked them about their experiences," she told Durango, "and they did start talking. And talking ... and talking."

Although based on her family, *Keoko* is a work of fiction that takes place in Korea in 1940. It is told from the perspective of a brother and sister, thirteen-year-old Tae-yul and ten-year-old Sun-hee, each of whom responds to their situation in very different ways. As World War II approaches, their lives are further threatened and their loyalty to family and country are increasingly challenged. It was a difficult story for Park to tell, and for her parents to revisit, but as she explained to Durango, "Your past is a huge part of what makes you you, and exploring the past can help you better understand the present and future."

# Future possibilities

In the mid-2000s Park continued to explore Korea's past and present in several new books that were aimed at a younger audience. *The Fire-keeper's Son,* published in 2004, gave readers a look at Korea in the 1800s, while *Mung-Mung,* also published in 2004, was a foldout book that introduced very young readers to the world of animal sounds. (Mung-mung is Korean for woof-woof.) In addition, Park kept up a steady pace of travel, visiting libraries and giving book readings. Her schedule, however, was much less hectic than it had been immediately following her Newbery win, which meant she could spend more time at home in upstate New York, a home that she shares with her husband, two children, a dog, a hamster, and eight tadpoles. When Durango asked Park if there were more books on Korean history in store for readers, the author replied, "I feel like I've only dipped my big toe into the possibilities of stories from Korean history! Like most writers, I have a lot of other interests as well—I don't know yet which of those will lead to books, but I can't wait to find out!"

# For More Information

### Books

Park, Linda Sue. *The Kite Fighters.* New York: Clarion Books, 2000.

———. *Seesaw Girl.* New York: Clarion Books, 1999.

———. *A Single Shard.* New York: Clarion Books, 2001.

———. *When My Name was Keoko.* New York: Clarion Books, 2002.

### Periodicals

Scotto, Barbara. "Review of *Seesaw Girl.*" *School Library Journal* (September 1999): p. 228.

### Web Sites

Durango, Julie. "A New Book and a Newbery for Linda Sue Park." *By the Book* (April 23, 2002). http://www.geocities.com/juliadurango/btbpark2.html (accessed on July 23, 2004).

Durango, Julie. "Seesaws and Kites: An Interview with Linda Sue Park." *By the Book* (July 8, 2000). http://www.geocities.com/juliadurango/btbpark.html (accessed on July 23, 2004).

Goodnow, Cecelia. "A Moment with ... Linda Sue Park, Children's Author." *Seattle Post-Intelligencer* (March 17, 2003). http://seattlepi.nwsource.com/books/112580_mome17.shtml (accessed on July 26, 2004).

"Interview with Linda Sue Park." *Alsop Review.* http://www.alsopreview. com/aside/lsparkinterview.html (accessed on July 26, 2004).

*Linda Sue Park Official Web Site.* http://www.lspark.com (accessed on July 22, 2004).

"Linda Sue Park Who-File." *Time for Kids.* http://www.timeforkids.com/ TFK/specials/story/0,6079,199125,00.html (accessed on July 23, 2004).

"Q&A with Newbery Winner Linda Sue Park." *Writer's Digest Magazine.* http://www.writersdigest.com/articles/interview/linda_sue_park.asp?se condarycategory=Children's+Subhome+Page (accessed on July 23, 2004).

Smith, Cynthia Leitich. "Interview with Children's and YA Book Author Linda Sue Park" (March 2002). http://www.cynthialeitichsmith.com/ auth-illLindaSuePark.htm (accessed on July 26, 2004).

# Richard Parsons

Kevin Mazur/Wire Image.com.

*April 4, 1948 • Brooklyn, New York*

## Chairman and CEO, Time Warner

**B**usiness executive Richard Parsons has been called a teddy bear, a master diplomat, and a charmer, but perhaps the best description that has been applied to him is "friendly giant." Standing at 6 feet 4 inches, with broad shoulders, he is a physically impressive man who could fill any boardroom. But, in this case, Parsons sits at the helm of one of the largest media companies in the world, Time Warner. When Parsons was named chief executive officer (CEO) in 2002 and chairman in 2003, he became one of the most powerful executives in the United States, but he also inherited a mountain of problems. A 2001 merger between Internet icon America Online (AOL) and Time Warner, a leader in the entertainment industry, had proven to be a failed experiment. As a result, the company struggled to maintain its credibility, its stock prices tumbled, and it faced $27 billion in debt. By the mid-2000s, however, analysts reported that Time Warner was on a definite upswing: employee morale was high, investors were newly confident, and the monstrous debt had been significantly slashed. And most

U·X·L newsmakers • volume 3

**561**

agreed that friendly giant Richard Parsons had been just what the frac-
tured titan needed.

## The Rockefeller Republican

Although Richard Dean Parsons regularly makes *Fortune* magazine's
annual list of the most powerful people in business, and he is considered to be one of the most respected African American executives in
the country, he came from an average working-class background. He
was born on April 4, 1948, in the Bedford-Stuyvesant section of
Brooklyn, New York, and was raised in the New York borough of

> **"I always knew I'd rise to the top; it never occurred to me that I couldn't."**

Queens. Parsons, however, was an extremely bright young man, who
went on to graduate from high school when he was just sixteen years
old. After graduation, he attended college at the University of Hawaii,
where he excelled both academically and socially; Parsons was a var-
sity basketball player and the social chairman of his fraternity. While
in Hawaii, he also met his future wife, Laura Bush.

Parsons had no clear idea what direction to take after college,
but at the prompting of Laura, he decided to go to law school. According to Bush, it was the most logical decision since Parsons enjoyed
arguing so much. Apparently it was the right decision. Parsons
worked part-time as a janitor to pay his way through the University of
Albany Law School in New York, and when he graduated in 1971, it
was at the top of his class. That same year, he scored the highest
marks out of the nearly four thousand lawyers who took the New York
State bar examination.

Just twenty-three years old, and fresh out of law school, Parsons
landed a job as an aide on the legal staff of Nelson Rockefeller
(1908–1979), the governor of New York. He became such a trusted
adviser that in 1974, when Rockefeller headed to Washington to serve

as vice president, Parsons was invited along. In Washington, the young lawyer also worked directly with President Gerald Ford (1913–), first as general counsel and then as an associate director of the domestic council. Thanks in part to such associations Parsons became what he frequently describes as a Rockefeller Republican, a person who is conservative when it comes to economic matters, and more liberal concerning social issues. For example, during his Washington years, the social-minded Parsons was chairman of the Wildcat Service Corporation, an organization that provides job training for people who have difficulty finding work because of past criminal records, addictions, or poverty.

## Lawyer turned banker

Parsons's tenure with Rockefeller and Ford opened up many doors for him and brought him to nationwide attention as an up-and-coming young executive. So, in 1976, when President Ford lost his re-election bid to Jimmy Carter (1924–), Parsons did not lack for opportunities. In 1977, he returned to New York, and at the request of former U.S. Deputy Attorney General Harold R. Tyler Jr., he joined the law firm of Patterson, Belknap, Webb & Tyler. He quickly became a star in the firm and in just two years was named partner. In his eleven years with Patterson, Parsons cemented his reputation as a skilled negotiator. He also expanded his web of connections, taking on such high-profile clients as Happy Rockefeller (1926–), the widow of Nelson Rockefeller, and cosmetics giant Estée Lauder. In addition, Parsons provided legal counsel to several major U.S. corporations, including the Dimes Savings Bank of New York, the largest savings and loan institution in the state.

In 1988, just when it seemed that Parsons was poised to become head of his law firm, the news was announced that he had accepted the position of chief operating officer (COO) of the Dime. In doing so, he became the first African American to head a lending institution of such proportion. Many, however, questioned the appointment since Parsons had no real experience in the banking industry. Skeptics also wondered how Parsons would fare in his new job considering the bank was facing financial ruin. As a result of the savings and loan crisis of the mid-1980s, the Dime had lost some $92.3 million; it was also under scrutiny from federal regulators.

Parsons lost no time in putting his years of Washington deal-making into action. He also set out to streamline the bank's operations. As part of his management restructure, Parsons opted to lay off almost one-third of the Dime's staff. It was a drastic move, but he also kept communications open with his employees every step of the way. As a result, Parsons became known as the consummate gentleman executive. "He is a persuader, not a dictator," a former colleague told CNET News.com. "He intellectualizes outcomes and gets people to agree with his outcomes." His tactics paid off, and in just a few years, Parsons had reduced the amount of the Dime's bad debts from $1 billion to $335 million.

After taking on the job of chairman and chief executive officer (CEO) of the Dime in 1990, Parsons continued to set the bank on its comeback course. In fact, in 1995 he was key in orchestrating the successful merger between the Dime and Anchor Savings Bank. As a result, Dime Bancorp became the largest thrift institution on the East Coast and the fourth largest in the United States. With the bank on solid ground, Parsons set his sights on a new enterprise.

## Banker becomes media mogul

In 1994, Gerald Levin (1939–), chairman of Time Warner (TW), openly recruited Parsons to take over as president of the company. Again, the business community was rocked by the news. True, Parsons had proven to be flexible enough to succeed in the banking world, but he had absolutely no background in media and entertainment. Many doubted that he could succeed at Time Warner, which was considered to be a media giant, controlling virtually all aspects of the industry, including television (CNN, HBO, Turner Classic Movies, WB Network); film (Warner Brothers, New Line Cinema); publishing (magazines such as *Time, People,* and *Sports Illustrated*); and music (Warner Music Group). Levin, however, felt that Parsons was the right man for the job, and some business insiders were not that surprised. After all, Parsons had sat on the company's board of directors for several years, and had developed close ties with top TW executives.

Parsons assumed his post as president of Time Warner in January of 1995, a job that came with a reported multi-million dollar salary. For the next six years, he served as the number-two executive at the company, and as Gerald Levin's right-hand man. Although Levin was effectively in charge, it was Parsons who consistently took on the tough assignments and it was Parsons who employees turned to for guidance. "Whenever we had a problem with one of the units, Parsons was always the guy who would solve it," former co-chairman of Warner Brothers Robert Daly explained to *Business Week*. "And he would do it in a way that everyone would feel good about the outcome." In addition, any time that trouble reared its head over regulatory issues in Washington, Parsons came to the rescue by turning to one of his many political contacts.

Time Warner faced its biggest challenge in 2000 when it announced plans to merge with America Online (AOL), which by the late 1990s had evolved into the nation's leading Internet provider.

*Richard Parsons poses with Bugs Bunny in 2004.* AP/Wide World Photo. Reproduced by permission.

Levin had been in negotiations with Steve Case (1958–), AOL's CEO, for several years. The hope was that by combining forces they would make the most successful merger in history: AOL would have access to Time Warner's massive media content and it would be able to reach even more users thanks to TW's cable television operations. In turn, Time Warner would have unlimited access to the ever-expanding Internet pipeline. The merger was made official in 2001, when AOL purchased Time Warner for a reported $168 billion. It did make history as the largest corporate purchase ever, but it also became known as perhaps the most failed megamerger on record.

After the deal was made, AOL Time Warner's board responsibilities were split directly in half, with one exception: Levin became the sole CEO in charge of operations; Case retained a backseat role as chairman. Parsons took on the role of co-COO, sharing the job with Robert Pittman (1953–), former president of AOL. To many, it seemed that Pittman took on most of the plum assignments in the company, considering he was in charge of the high-profile AOL operations. But it was Parsons who oversaw the units that brought in the most revenue, including Warner Brothers, New Line Cinema, and Time Warner Trade Publishing. He was also in charge of the legal department and human resources. Still, when Levin announced, in late 2001, that he would be leaving AOL Time Warner, the assumption was that Pittman would be his likely successor.

## AOL Time Warner struggles

In a December 2001 press conference, Levin stunned the industry when he named Parsons as AOL Time Warner's next CEO. As reported in *Jet* magazine, Levin commented, "I have the greatest confidence in Dick Parsons' ability to lead the company forward, coalesce its diverse interests, and work with our strategic partners to achieve our ambitious goals." Once again, Parsons made history, becoming what Adam Cohen of *Time* called the "first African American to lead the world's most influential media company." The world's most influential media company, however, was struggling. AOL Time Warner's various operating units were still far from achieving a full integration. In addition, thanks to an industry-wide technology slump, AOL, which had promised big revenues, had failed to deliver. Just before Parsons officially took over from Levin in May of 2002, the company posted a quarterly loss of $54 billion, the largest in U.S. history.

Parsons remained optimistic, but he proceeded cautiously. As he told Cohen, "Ideally, you want to underpromise and overdeliver. To the extent that we've lost credibility, repairing it is important." Parsons's critics were not impressed by this middle-of-the-road philosophy, but his supporters pointed out that underlying the nice-guy image was a savvy businessman. As one AOL shareholder told *Business Week,* "Dick is the right guy to be running the company right now." In this case, Parsons was forced to tap into both sides of his personality. With a calm, cool-headed resolve, he doggedly tackled the problems that lay ahead.

When Robert Pittman stepped down as COO in June of 2002, Parsons quickly reorganized the company's top ranks by promoting some of Time Warner's former division chiefs. And, after taking over as chairman from Steve Case, who stepped down in January of 2003, Parsons went to work to repair the damage from the AOL merger. In mid-2003, he sold off parts of the company that were considered to be noncore assets, including the sports teams, the Atlanta Hawks and Atlanta Thrashers. In his biggest move to trim the $27 billion debt, Parsons sold Warner Music Group in November of 2003 for a reported $2.6 billion.

In spite of its debt, the company reported an overall increase in revenue (6 percent) in early 2004, thanks to three of the Time Warner divisions: film, cable, and network advertising. The biggest boost came from the film division, which had experienced an enormous success because of the Harry Potter and *The Lord of the Rings* series. The drag on the company continued to be AOL, which consistently floundered. In September of 2003, Parsons made a surprising announcement: AOL Time Warner was undergoing a name change, and would in the future be known as simply Time Warner. "Renaming our company will strengthen the identity of the AOL brand name among consumers," the CEO said in a written statement reported on CNN-Money.com. "America Online is an important part of our company and we expect it to continue to make major contributions to our success in the future."

## A giant of a role model

Analysts wondered about the future of AOL even as Parsons continued to play peacemaker, overseeing Monday morning meetings with his various managers and promising harmony between teams. "It's a collaboration," he told Anthony Bianco and Tom Lowry of *Business Week*. "Getting your team together is the more important thing." At the same time people speculated about what role Parsons would play in Time Warner's future. In the same *Business Week* interview, the CEO revealed, "I take this job seriously. It's important I do it well.... But it's not my life. I exist apart from this job."

Some predicted a future in politics for Parsons. In addition to his work for Rockefeller and the Ford administration, the lawyer-turned-banker-turned media executive served in various political roles throughout his career. When Rudolph Giuliani (1944–) was elected mayor of New York in 1993, Parsons headed his transitional council; he served on the transition team when Michael Bloomberg (1942–) became the mayor of New York in 2001; and that same year, he was named co-chair of President George W. Bush's Social Security Commission. Parsons also remained a committed leader in other areas of public and community service. He serves on the board of several cultural institutions, including the Museum of Modern Art and Lincoln Center. He also serves as chairman of the Upper Manhattan Empowerment Zone Development Corporation, which was established to spur the development of business and the growth of job opportunities in Harlem.

Whether he remains with Time Warner or runs for public office, or goes in a totally different direction, Parsons will continue to be a role model in the African American community. He frequently downplays race as a factor or handicap in his success. As he once told the *New York Times,* as reported by CNNMoney.com, "For a lot of people race is a defining issue. It just isn't for me. It is … like air. It's like height. I have other things I'm focused on." Regardless, Parsons is consistently applauded by various groups for the inspiration he provides to young people everywhere. In 2004, he was awarded the Better Chance Corporate Award, an annual honor bestowed by the organization A Better Chance, which, according to Hispanic PRWire, "identifies, recruits, and develops leaders among academically gifted students of color." According to Better Chance president Sandra Timmons, as quoted by Hispanic PRWire, "Richard Parsons serves as a role model for aspiring executives of all races, but his success has earned him a special leadership role among African Americans."

## For More Information

### Periodicals

Cohen, Adam. "Can a Nice Guy Run This Thing?" *Time* (December 17, 2001).

Hayden, Thomas. "The Man Who Keeps the Peace: AOL Time-Warner's Richard Parsons." *Newsweek* (January 24, 2000): p. 36.

McClellan, Steve. "AOL Time Warner Still Fixing Holes." *Broadcasting & Cable* (July 28, 2003): p. 8.

Mehta, Stephanie. "Richard Parsons: Profile." *Fortune* (August 8, 2004).

"Reeling Like a Bad Movie: AOL Time Warner." *The Economicst* (April 19, 2003).

"Richard D. Parsons Named New CEO of AOL Time Warner." *Jet* (December 24, 2001): p. 6.

### Web Sites

Bianco, Anthony, and Tom Lowry. "Can Dick Parsons Rescue AOL Time Warner?" *BusinessWeek Online* (May 19, 2003) http://www.business week.com/magazine/content/03_20/b3833001_mz001.htm (accessed on July 29, 2004).

Hu, Jim. "Parsons Faces Major Test in Unifying AOL Time Warner." *CNET News.com* (April 3, 2002) http://news.com.com/2009-1023-873910.html (accessed on July 29, 2004).

Isidore, Chris. "Time Warner Drops AOL Name." *CNNMoney.com.* (September 18, 2003) http://money.cnn.com/2003/09/18/technology/aol_name (accessed on July 31, 2004).

"Parsons the Man: Public Service as Much as Private Sector Success Define AOL Time Warner's New CEO." *CNNMoney.com* (December 5, 2001) http://money.cnn.com/2001/12/05/ceos/parsons_profile (accessed on July 29, 2004).

"Time Warner's Chairman and CEO Richard D. Parsons Honored by a Better Chance." *Hispanic PRWire* (June 11, 2004) http://www.hispanicprwire.com/news_in.php?id=2478&cha=6&PHPSESSID (accessed on July 31, 2004).

# Nancy Pelosi

*March 26, 1940* • *Baltimore, Maryland*

Politician

**N**ancy Pelosi is the first woman in American history to lead a political party in Congress. She has served the U.S. House of Representatives since 1987, when voters in San Francisco chose her to represent them in Washington. In 2002 her fellow Democratic Party lawmakers voted to make her House minority leader. She is the first woman ever to hold such a post. Republicans sometimes call Pelosi a "latte liberal" for her politically progressive views on the environment, women's reproductive rights, labor unions, and other issues. Pelosi has been outspoken in her criticism of President George W. Bush (1946–).

## The mayor's daughter

Nancy Pelosi began her career in politics at a young age. Her father, Thomas "Tommy" J. D'Alesandro Jr., was a popular local politician from the Little Italy section of Baltimore, Maryland. Just a year before Pelosi was born, her father won election to the same U.S. House of Representatives in which she would serve many years later.

Pelosi was born Nancy Patricia D'Alesandro on March 26, 1940, in Baltimore. She was the last of six children, and the first daughter. The family lived on Albemarle Street in Little Italy. Their neighborhood was a loyal Democratic Party stronghold in Maryland politics. Little Italy was a working class and largely Roman Catholic neighborhood, located near the city's main harbor. The local church, St. Leo's, and the nearby Democratic Party office were the centers of social and economic life for Italian-American families.

Pelosi's father was well-known in Little Italy, and went on to become a Baltimore legend. When she was seven years old, he became the city's first Italian-American mayor. He served three terms, and so Pelosi was known as the mayor's daughter for most of her

> **"Any one of us who decides to put our young people in harm's way carries a responsibility for the consequences."**

childhood and teens. She often worked on his campaigns, as did her five brothers. In 1952, when Pelosi was just twelve years old, she was allowed to attend her first Democratic National Convention, where delegates choose their party's presidential candidate.

Pelosi's family were dedicated Democrats, and her parents were strict Roman Catholics as well. For a son or daughter to enter one of the Church's religious orders was considered a great honor for the family. Not surprisingly, her mother hoped that her daughter might do so, but Pelosi was not interested. "I didn't think I wanted to be a nun, but I thought I might want to be a priest because there seemed to be a little more power there," she said years later in an interview with Joe Feuerherd of the *National Catholic Reporter*.

## Five children in six years

During the 1950s many devout Roman Catholic families placed restrictions on their children, and Pelosi's early family life was no different. She attended the Institute of Notre Dame High School in Baltimore, a school for young women. When it came time to choose a college, her parents permitted her to travel only as far as Washington, D.C., which was less than fifty miles from Baltimore. She entered Trinity College, a Roman Catholic college for women. It was an entirely new world for her. For someone who had grown up in Little Italy, she compared it to "going to Australia with a backpack," as she joked in a *People* interview with journalist J. D. Heyman.

Pelosi earned her degree from Trinity in 1962, and then served as a congressional intern for a Maryland senator. She thought about law school, but followed the more traditional path for a young woman of her era, that of marriage. Her husband, Paul Pelosi, was a recent Georgetown University graduate and a native of San Francisco. The couple settled in the New York City area, where Pelosi' new husband worked as a banker. She began raising a family, and was the mother of five by 1969, the same year the family moved across the country to San Francisco.

Pelosi was a homemaker for a number of years. Her youngest daughter, Alexandra, told *People* that she and her siblings were not an easy crew: "We were like the kids from The Simpsons—she couldn't get anyone to babysit." No matter how busy she was at home, Pelosi always volunteered for the Democratic party during election campaigns. In 1976 she worked for the presidential campaign of California's popular governor, Jerry Brown (1938–). Because of her political connections back in Maryland, she was asked to organize a "Brown for President" campaign there. Brown went on to win an unexpected primary victory in Maryland, thanks to Pelosi. Later that year he lost the Democratic Party's presidential nomination to Georgia's governor, Jimmy Carter (1947–).

The experience boosted Pelosi's reputation as a behind-the-scenes dynamo. In 1977 she became chair for the northern section of the California Democratic Party, and four years later became the chair for the entire state. She later served in a national party post as the finance chair for the 1986 congressional elections. Known for her top skills in recruiting candidates and getting them elected, Pelosi had never considered running for office herself. That changed when one of her longtime political allies was diagnosed with cancer and suggested that Pelosi run for the seat in the coming special election. It was not a local or state office—it was for a seat in the U.S. House of Representatives.

## Daughter Films Bush on Campaign Trail

Nancy Pelosi's youngest daughter, Alexandra, is a journalist and filmmaker who brought a camcorder with her when she covered the 2000 presidential election for NBC News. Pelosi wanted to document what the campaign looked like from her seat on the bus that carried the press corps. The result was a fascinating behind-the-scenes documentary film, *Journeys with George.*

Alexandra Pelosi was born in 1969 and grew up in a family that regularly pitched in to help during Democratic political campaigns. She graduated from Loyola Marymount College in Los Angeles in 1991, and went to work for NBC News after attending graduate school at the University of Southern California. She was a producer for *Dateline,* and then covered Congress for the network. In early 2000 she was named to the campaign press corps team and assigned to the bus that followed Texas Governor George W. Bush around the country in his bid for the Republican nomination.

Pelosi's camcorder captured a side of the candidate that was rarely seen in regular news coverage. He joked with the journalists, though he sometimes criticized their reporting, liked to eat Cheeze Doodles, and played with a Magic 8 Ball. He even asked it to predict the election results, and the answer came back, "Outlook not so good." Bush even suggested the film's title to Pelosi. "My mother used to rip his father's policies on the House floor," Pelosi said in a *WWD* interview with Rosemary Feitelberg. It gave her and the Texas governor some unusual common ground, she felt. "I covered [Capitol] Hill for six years," she pointed out. "I have an

## San Francisco's Washington voice

Pelosi won the 1987 special election as well as the next regular election in 1988. San Francisco voters regularly returned her to the seat, often by margins of 80 percent. As a member of Congress representing California's Eighth Congressional District, she served a population known as liberal and progressive, and she spoke for it in Congress. She argued for and won increased government funding for AIDS (Acquired Immune Deficiency Syndrome, which reduces the body's ability to fight off infection) research. The city had a disproportionately large number of residents who were HIV-positive (diagnosed with Human Immunodeficiency Virus, the virus that causes AIDS). There was a large Asian immigrant community in the city, and Pelosi made no secret of her distaste for a new American foreign policy that sought to forge new economic ties with China, which had been under authoritarian Communist Party rule for decades and was still accused of drastic violations of its citizens' human rights. In 1991, on a visit to the same Tiananmen Square where the Chinese army had killed protesters two years earlier, Pelosi held up a protest sign.

aversion to all that seriousness. I think he does, too. That's the irony."

After the election Pelosi quit her job at NBC and went to work editing the film in her New York City apartment. It aired on the HBO cable network just before her mother was elected House minority leader in the fall of 2002. The White House press office made a few rumbles about it, but quickly backed down from a fight. When Pelosi promoted the film she tried to stay away from talking about her own political views. "I come from a political family," she explained to Feitelberg. "I think you should let people make their own judgements." Other articles noted that she was indeed a liberal-leaning Democrat, much like her mother. But Pelosi insisted that her goal in making the film was to make a kind of home movie. "I do think you shouldn't vote for someone who you wouldn't feel comfortable having

*Nancy Pelosi (left) and her daughter Alexandra Pelosi, pose with a poster for Alexandra's documentary,* Journeys with George. Arun Nevader/Wirelmage.com.

in your living room," she said in the *WWD* interview. "Some people think this humanizes him and makes him look like a fun person to go on a road trip with. Others say it confirms their worst suspicions."

Pelosi's leadership abilities emerged in the mid-1990s, when Republicans gained a majority in the U.S. House of Representatives for the first time in forty years. Many of the new Republican legislators were drastically conservative in their views. For example, some believed that the federal government should promote a healthy economy by reducing the financial penalties that corporations paid for polluting the environment. In response Pelosi began to assume a more public profile in opposing their legislation. In October of 2001 she was elected as minority whip in the House, when a vacancy arose. The whip's job was to make certain that Democrats, who were in the "minority" among the 435 lawmakers in the House of Representatives, would vote with their party on specific pieces of legislation. She also worked to find Republican legislators willing to cross party lines and vote with Democrats on certain issues. Pelosi became the first woman to hold such a post in Congress.

A year later Pelosi won another important first when House minority leader Richard A. Gephardt stepped down from the job. In this job Gephardt had served as the official leader of the Democrats in the House of Representatives. Pelosi ran for the post against fellow lawmaker Harold Ford Jr. of Tennessee, but House Democrats chose Pelosi by a vote of 177 to 29. As House minority leader, Pelosi led the 206 Democrats in opposing various policies of the Republican White House and Congress. She was an outspoken critic of President Bush's economic policies, and also voiced concerns about a planned war in Iraq.

## The "latte" liberal

On other matters Pelosi emerged as a progressive voice inside a party that had begun to take a more moderate political tone during the 1990s. She is still critical of China because of its human rights record, and supports women's reproductive rights. Her Republican counterparts often refer to her as a "San Francisco Democrat," which is a code word in conservative politics for someone who is ultra-liberal.

In the spring of 2004 the year-old American-led occupation of Iraq had become increasingly deadly on both sides. In May, U.S. military planes attacked a rural gathering that was said to have been a wedding celebration, and forty Iraqi civilians died. In her regular weekly press conference, Pelosi issued harsh words for the president. "Bush is an incompetent leader," the *San Francisco Chronicle*'s Marc Sandalow quoted her as saying. "In fact, he's not a leader. He's a person who has no judgment, no experience and no knowledge of the subjects that he has to decide upon." She asserted that U.S. soldiers were ill-equipped, despite the several billion dollars in funds that Congress had approved. She noted, for example, that parents of soldiers were sending their sons and daughters Kevlar lining, a bullet-resistant material that the Pentagon had not issued to all personnel.

## Poised to take another first

Pelosi also predicted that Bush would not win election to a second term in November of 2004 because of the war, which she estimated might end up costing U.S. taxpayers as much as $250 billion. A Democratic victory in November could give Pelosi's party a majority in the House once again. In that case, she might become the new Speaker of the House, or the floor leader of the majority party. The position would make her third in the line of presidential succession, after the vice president. Pelosi's name was also mentioned as a possible vice presidential candidate for Democratic Party candidate John Kerry (1943–). Kerry selected North Carolina senator John Edwards (1943–) as his running mate in July of 2004.

Known in Washington for her ready smile and stylish suits, the grandmother of five puts in long hours at work. Staffers claim they can hear their boss coming down the hallways by the rapid "click-click" of her heels. "As the first woman to lead a party in Congress, Ms. Pelosi, elegant and energetic, has the kind of star quality that many say makes them again excited to be Democrats," noted *New York Times* writer Sheryl Gay Stolberg. Pelosi claims she does take time out to relax, sometimes at a Napa Valley home she shares with her husband. Completing the challenging *New York Times* crossword puzzle is one of her favorite hobbies.

## For More Information

### *Periodicals*

Chaddock, Gail Russell and Mark Sappenfield. "Pelosi Shatters a Marble Ceiling." *Christian Science Monitor* (November 14, 2002): p. 1.

Clymer, Adam. "A New Vote Counter—Nancy Patricia Pelosi." *New York Times* (October 11, 2001): p. A18.

Feitelberg, Rosemary. "Showtime for Pelosi and Curious George." *WWD* (March 5, 2002): p. 15

Feuerherd, Joe. "Roots in Faith, Family and Party Guide Pelosi's Move to Power." *National Catholic Reporter* (January 24, 2003): p. 3.

Feuerherd, Joe. "The Gospel in a Catholic's Political Life." *National Catholic Reporter* (January 24, 2003): p. 4.

Firestone, David. "Getting Closer to the Top, and Smiling All the Way." *New York Times* (November 10, 2002): p. 30.

Heyman, J. D. "House Proud: Adept at Both Politics and Politesse, Democrat Nancy Pelosi Becomes the Most Powerful Woman in Congress." *People* (December 2, 2002): p. 217.

Samuel, Terence. "She's Cracking the Whip." *U.S. News & World Report* (June 17, 2002): p. 18.

Sandalow, Marc. "Nancy Pelosi / Holding Out for Dreams." *San Francisco Chronicle* (June 9, 1996): p. 3/Z1.

Sandalow, Marc. "U.S. Kills 40 Civilians in Village Attack." *San Francisco Chronicle* (May 20, 2004): p. A1.

Stolberg, Sheryl Gay. "With Democrats Divided on War, Pelosi Faces Leadership Test." *New York Times* (April 1, 2003): p. B13.

"Transcript of Today's Pelosi Press Conference." *America's Intelligence Wire* (May 20, 2004).

Tresniowski, Alex. "Bush Tracker: George W. Bush Untamed! Filmmaker Alexandra Pelosi Captures the Candid Candidate." *People* (March 25, 2002): p. 89.

# Michael Phelps

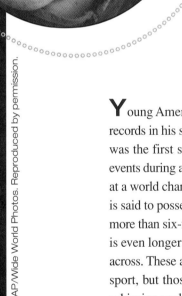

*June 30, 1985 • Baltimore, Maryland*

## Swimmer

**Y**oung American swimmer Michael Phelps has broken several world records in his sport. Even his record breaking has broken new records: he was the first swimmer ever to shatter two world records in individual events during a single day, and was the first to swim five new fastest times at a world championship meet. Phelps, whose best stroke is the butterfly, is said to possess the perfect build for competitive swimming. He stands more than six-foot four inches in height, and his wingspan, as it is called, is even longer: from finger to finger he measures six-foot seven inches across. These attributes have given him an edge in the highly competitive sport, but those who know him say that it is his inner drive, focus on achieving goals, and likeable personality that make him a winner.

## Discovered Olympic potential

Phelps was born on June 30, 1985, and grew up in the Baltimore suburb of Towson. His mother, Debbie, is an administrator with the Baltimore County school system. He has two older sisters, and began swimming when they joined a local swim team. "At first, I was a little scared to put my head underwater, so I started with the backstroke," Phelps told Frank Litsky, a sportswriter for the *New York Times*, adding, "I was still scared because I don't think I had goggles."

Phelps's parents quickly recognized their son's talent. When he was eleven years old, they brought him to a top swim coach, Bob Bowman (c. 1964–). After watching him swim, Bowman agreed to take over his training at a Baltimore-area swim club. Bowman predicted that Phelps would be Olympic-caliber material by the time he was fifteen, and might look forward to going to the 2000 Summer Games

**"It's when your body is not in the best situation, your mind is not in the best situation and things are against you those are the times that really count and really matter you overcome and rise to the occasion."**

in Sydney, Australia. Phelps was thrilled by the idea, especially since one of his sisters had qualified for the U.S. women's swim team at the 1996 Summer Games but was sidelined by an injury.

When Bowman told Phelps that he had Olympic potential, the twelve-year-old gave up his other sports, which were soccer, lacrosse, and baseball, in order to bring all his energy to daily pool practice. He began winning every competitive event he entered. The first time he lost, however, he was so upset that he threw down his goggles. Bowman warned him about his unsportsmanlike conduct, and since then Phelps has taken his handful of setbacks in stride.

Those setbacks included his first-ever U.S. national championships, in the summer of 1999. He finished in last place in the 200-meter butterfly. He bounced back at the 2000 U.S. spring nationals to take a third place finish, and then became a surprise qualifier for the

## Swim Legend Mark Spitz

At the 1972 Summer Olympic Games in Munich, Germany, a young California athlete by the name of Mark Spitz became an international celebrity and Olympic legend. Brash, confident, and phenomenally fast, Spitz beat out the other world-caliber swimmers to win seven gold medals in the sport. No other athlete has ever attained such a feat during a single Olympics.

Born in 1950, Spitz was a talented swimmer in his teens, much like Michael Phelps. Before he competed in the 1968 Summer Olympic Games in Mexico City, Spitz predicted he would win six gold medals, but went home with just two. His confidence was viewed by some as arrogant and unsportsmanlike, and he said little after returning to an intense training schedule for the 1972 Olympics.

But Spitz became the star of the Munich Summer Games. He won his first gold medal in the 200-meter butterfly, setting a world record. He went on to enter six other events, and set world records in each of them. In just eight days he set seven world records and won seven gold medals, including one for the 100-meter freestyle, which was considered his weakest stroke. No other Olympic athlete has ever accomplished such a feat, in either Winter or Summer events.

During the second week of the Games, a group of hooded men associated with an Arab political organization took several Israeli athletes hostage in the Olympic Village. They demanded that Israel release Palestinian prisoners in return. The standoff ended tragically with a botched rescue attempt. The nine Israeli men died, as did several of the hostage takers. Spitz was forced to leave Munich earlier than planned because of the crisis—he was Jewish, and Olympic officials were worried about his safety.

Spitz enjoyed lucrative endorsement contracts after his Munich performance. His dark good looks and mustache made him an early 1970s heartthrob, and he was one of the first Olympic athletes to earn a small fortune from such contracts.

Sydney Olympics later that year. When he arrived with the rest of the U.S. swim team, he was the youngest American male swimmer to enter an Olympic contest since 1932. He had qualified for just one event, the 200-meter butterfly, and finished in fifth place.

## Began setting new records

A few months later, in early 2001, Phelps surprised everyone once again. At the U.S. spring nationals, he became the youngest male swimmer to set a world record. The event that marked this accomplishment was the 200-meter butterfly. He was just fifteen years and nine months old at the time. At the age of sixteen, he decided to give up his chances for a college athletic scholarship by signing an endorsement deal with swimsuit maker Speedo.

Phelps soon began breaking world records in every event he entered. In August of 2002, at the U.S. National Swimming Championships in Fort Lauderdale, Florida, he set a world record in the 400-meter individual medley. The following April, at the 2003 U.S. spring nationals hosted by Indiana University, he beat his own world record in the 400-meter individual medley. *Rocky Mountain News* journalist Jody Berger wrote that Phelps "flies across a pool like water is someone else's problem. He doesn't punch his way through the wet stuff but hydroplanes across its surface at a speed few humans can match."

The official Indiana meet was followed by a special contest between American and Australian swimmers billed as the "Duel in the Pool." The United States and Australia have each produced several top swimmers in the modern era of the sport, and there is an intense national rivalry between the two countries. But Phelps's biggest rival, Australian champion Ian Thorpe (1982–), was ill with meningitis-like symptoms and did not compete, creating much interest in what would happen in a contest between the two swimmers at the World Championships in Barcelona, Spain, in July of 2003.

*Micheal Phelps competes in the 200-meter mens' butterfly event of the 2003 FINA World Swimming Championship in Spain.* AP/Wide World Photos. Reproduced by permission.

Thorpe, three years older than Phelps, is a huge star in Australia. Sportswriters there call him "Thorpedo." He won three gold medals at the 2000 Sydney Games, and was also a world record holder. Their rivalry heated up in June of 2003, when Thorpe's coach told the press that Phelps was not yet a serious threat. "The promise with Phelps is there, but for people saying he's going to outdo Thorpie, I live to see that day," *Sports Illustrated* writer Brian Cazeneuve quoted coach Don Talbot as saying.

## Called the next Mark Spitz

Phelps bested Thorpe in nearly every contest in Barcelona in late July of 2003, and it made the American the new star in competitive swimming. He won five medals and set an astonishing five world records. The first came in the 100-meter butterfly semifinal, and the next came when he broke his own record in the 200-meter individual medley, besting Thorpe by a large margin in that contest. His own American teammate, Ian Crocker (1982–), broke Phelps's 100-meter butterfly record in the finals, but Phelps went on to take part in two relay races that each won a gold medal. His last two world records were set in the 400-meter individual medley and the 200-meter butterfly.

Phelps was seemingly unstoppable. Just a short time later, at the U.S. summer nationals in College Park, Maryland, he won five of the fourteen gold medals awarded, becoming the first male swimmer ever to do that at a U.S. nationals event. With such a promising start, the eighteen-year-old was called the next Mark Spitz (1950–). Phelps had heard the name before, as he recalled in an interview with Elliott Almond that appeared in the Knight Ridder/Tribune News Service. He told Almond that he asked his coach, "'Why are they asking me about Mark Spitz? What did he do?'" he told Almond. Bowman explained to him that Spitz was an American swimmer who was the star athlete of the 1972 Summer Olympic Games in Munich, Germany. Spitz set seven world records in Munich, and returned home with seven gold medals.

Phelps's interest in matching Spitz's legendary performance intensified when Thorpe asserted that no one could ever repeat Spitz's feat. Late in 2003 Phelps signed a new contract with Speedo that showed the company's faith in him: it ran until 2009, and included a

$1 million bonus if he matched Spitz's seven gold medals at the coming 2004 Summer Olympics in Athens, Greece. In the buildup before the Athens Games, Phelps was predicted to become the star American athlete. But he tried not to make any predictions. "If you get caught up in it, your mind will take over and control you," told Litsky in a *New York Times* article. "I have to make sure I'm in control."

Phelps did not worry about the other problems he might face at the Athens Games. In one interview Phelps was asked if he was concerned that the roof over the new Olympic pool had not been completed with only three months to go before the Games' opening ceremonies. It would not matter to him or to his performance, he told Duncan Goodhew in the *Financial Times*. "A pool's a pool. Water, lane lines, starting blocks," he remarked. "We are all in the same boat. We all swim under the same sun." Phelps did not match Spitz's record, but he did take home six gold medals and two bronze medals.

## Uses rap songs to focus

Phelps is known for his perseverance and concentration in the pool. He swims twenty thousand meters on some days. Kevin Clements, a friend at the Baltimore area club where Phelps practices, told the *New York Times*'s Litsky that Phelps "likes to train. He's never satisfied. Outside the pool, he's a normal guy to hang out with. He likes to tease and fool around with other people on the team, which is natural in this atmosphere. But he's mature in ways, too. He kind of makes training fun."

Rap music helps Phelps focus on his goals. Before every meet, he swims his warmup laps, then changes into a new swimsuit and puts his headphones on for the entire thirty-minute period before the race is set to start. He likes Snoop Dogg, 50 Cent, and Eminem. He also listens to music every day while he drives to practice. "When I get out of the car, the last song stays in my head," he explained to *Dallas Morning News* journalist Cathy Harasta, in an article that appeared in the Knight Ridder/Tribune News Service. "It's there all during practice, in my head."

His car is a Cadillac Escalade sport utility vehicle, which he bought used with the $25,000 bonus he earned from the U.S. Swimming Federation when he began breaking world records in 2003. His mother allows him to buy something with his winnings every time he sets a new world record. One treat was a 47-inch television for his bedroom. Another time, he installed new subwoofer speakers in the Escalade, to create a better bass sound for his favorite rap songs.

## Headed to University of Michigan

Phelps graduated from Towson High School in 2003, but delayed college plans to concentrate on training for the 2004 Olympics. In April of 2004, Bowman was hired as the new men's swim coach at the University of Michigan, which had produced several top athletes in the sport over the years. Phelps was not allowed to swim for the school because he had turned professional by accepting the Speedo endorsement in 2001. He went out and bought two U-M caps for himself and for Bowman, however, and planned to enroll there as a student so they could continue to train. In 2004 he said that he plans to swim for another ten years.

In his spare time Phelps likes to play video games. He makes appearances for Speedo and also serves as the national spokesperson for the Boys & Girls Clubs of America. Later in life, he has said, he would like to have a career in either sports marketing or in some technical field. He told Goodhew he hoped his own success as a champion swimmer would boost the sport's profile. "One of my big goals is to improve the knowledge of the sport. Not many people know about swimming and (I want) to be able to take it to a new level and hopefully, in the US, get in with sports like basketball (or) football, where people see (swimmers) on the street and know who they are."

## For More Information

*Periodicals*

Ackert, Kristie. "Phelps Wins Sullivan Award." Knight Ridder/Tribune News Service (April 13, 2004): p. K5446.

Almond, Elliott. "Swimmer Phelps Vying for Lucky Seven." Knight Ridder/Tribune News Service (May 22, 2004): p. K4972.

Barnas, Jo-Ann. "Bowman Named U-M Swim Coach." Knight Ridder/Tribune News Service (April 2, 2004): p. K6521.

Berger, Jody. "Phelps Toys with Competition: U.S. Swimmer Has Eyes on Collection of Olympic Medals." *Rocky Mountain News* (April 5, 2003): p. 16B.

Cazeneuve, Brian. "World Beater: Teenage Sensation Michael Phelps Dominated the World Championships." *Sports Illustrated* (August 4, 2003): p. 74.

DeArmond, Mike. "Phelps: 'I'm Nowhere Near Perfect.'" Knight Ridder/Tribune News Service (May 16, 2004): p. K1670.

Goodhew, Duncan. "Phelps Ready to Make an Almighty Splash." *Financial Times* (May 19, 2004): p. 14.

Harasta, Cathy. "In Chasing Spitz, Phelps Could Sparkle in Olympic Limelight." Knight Ridder/Tribune News Service (May 4, 2004): p. K1690.

Hersh, Philip. "Phelps Eyeing Spitz's Record." Knight Ridder/Tribune News Service (February 11, 2004): p. K5980.

Kelly, Dan. "How to Build a Champion: These Four Teenage Athletes Have What It Takes to Succeed in Sports—And in Life." *Boys' Life* (March 2002): p. 26.

Layden, Tim. "A Real Gold-Getter: Heading into the Olympic year, 18-year-old Michael Phelps Lowered Five World Records and Raised Expectations to Positively Spitzian Levels." *Sports Illustrated* (December 29, 2003): p. Z16 (Special).

Litsky, Frank. "American Nearly Wins Meet by Himself." *New York Times* (April 7, 2003): p. D2.

———. "Good Morning, Mr. Phelps. Next Mission: Olympics." *New York Times* (February 16, 2004): p. D10.

———. "Phelps Sets His Sights On Spitz's Achievement." *New York Times* (February 11, 2004): p. D4.

———. "Youngster Quickly Joins Elite." *New York Times* (November 30, 2001): p. S7.

Lord, Craig. "Phelps Puts Brake on Thorpedo but Spitz Hype Dims; Swimming: World Championships." *Times* (London, England) (July 28, 2003): p. 34.

Noden, Merrell. "Catching Up With … Mark Spitz." *Sports Illustrated* (August 4, 1997): p. 11.

### Web Sites

*NBCOlympics.com.* http://www.nbcolympics.com/swimming/index.html (accessed on September 2, 2004).

# *Queer Eye* for the *Straight Guy* Cast

**B**ravo Television's *Queer Eye for the Straight Guy* is a reality makeover show that became the surprise television hit of 2003. In each episode the "Fab Five" team of five gay men make a visit to a heterosexual man's home. They redecorate it, take him shopping for a new wardrobe, provide grooming tips and date suggestions, and teach him how to cook a meal that will wow his girlfriend, wife, or party guests. The five specialists are Ted Allen, Kyan Douglas, Thom Filicia, Carson Kressley, and Jai Rodriguez. Each became an overnight celebrity after the show debuted in the summer of 2003.

## Who are the "Fab Five"?

## Ted Allen
### *1965 • Indiana*
### Television host

Each cast member of *Queer Eye for the Straight Guy* brings his own area of expertise to the show. Food and wine expert Ted Allen is the oldest of the Fab Five. Born in 1965, he grew up in Carmel, Indiana, and was known to occasionally take over his family's kitchen for cooking projects. He settled in Chicago after college, where he wrote feature stories for *Chicago* magazine. In 1997 he was hired by *Esquire* magazine to be its food critic. He learned of the *Queer Eye* auditions when a friend of his in New York City called to tell him about it. "It cost $200 to fly to New York," Allen recalled in an inter-

Queer Eye for the Straight Guy cast, from left: Ted Allen, Carson Kressly, Jai Rodriguez, Thom Filicia, and Kyan Douglas. AP/Wide World Photos. Reproduced by permission.

view with *Crain's Chicago Business* writer Jeremy Mullman. "It just seemed like a lark at the time."

# Kyan Douglas

### *1970 • Florida*

## Television host

*Queer Eye*'s grooming guru Kyan Douglas is usually described as the most handsome of the Fab Five. A native of Tallahassee, Florida, Douglas was named "Edward" when he was born in 1970, but later changed his name to Kyan. As a teenager he experimented with making his own skin care products in a food processor at home. That interest in natural ingredients led him to Aveda, a line of plant-based hair and skin care products. He worked at the Aveda Institute as a certified cosmetologist before joining the staff of Manhattan's Arrojo Studio as a colorist. One of his clients suggested that he audition for *Queer Eye*.

# Thom Filicia

### *1969 • New York*

## Television host

Interior designer Thom Filicia grew up in the suburbs of Syracuse, New York. His father was an engineer and his mother sometimes took him along to the houses she was selling as a real estate broker. In 1976, when he was seven years old, his parents permitted Filicia to redecorate his bedroom in shades of orange and lime green. After he graduated from Syracuse University he worked at three Manhattan interior design firms before starting his own in 1998. In September of 2002 the elevator in his apartment building stalled, and he and his dog were stranded inside for a hour with another passenger. She was a talent manager, and called him the next day about auditioning for *Queer Eye*.

........................................................................................................

## "There are a lot of people in the rest of the world that aren't even familiar with the word queer being a positive word for us now. And being an inclusive word."

**Ted Allen, *Advocate* interview, September 3, 2003.**

# Carson Kressley

*1969 • Pennsylvania*

## Television host

Fashion stylist Carson Kressley quickly became the breakout star of the Fab Five, thanks to his quick wit. Born in 1969, he grew up in Allentown, Pennsylvania, and once helped his older sister pick out her prom dress. She went on to win the prom queen title. He studied finance and fine art at Gettysburg College, where he graduated magna cum laude. He was working as a freelance fashion stylist for Polo Ralph Lauren in New York City when a colleague told him about the *Queer Eye* auditions.

# Jai Rodriguez

*June 22, 1977 • Brentwood, New York*

## Television host

Born in 1977, Jai Rodriguez is the youngest of the cast. The "culture vulture" is sometimes described as the most underutilized Fab Five

## Behind the Scenes of *Queer Eye*

The makeover event shown on each episode of *Queer Eye for the Straight Guy* seems to happen in one day, but actually takes three or four to finish. The show usually opens with the experts in their sport utility vehicle, with its "Fab 5" vanity plate, as they are driving to surprise their next guest star. The dossier on the man, which they discuss on-camera, is generally all they have been told about their new client. Often the living quarters are even worse than expected. "People always ask us, 'Are the places really that bad when you get in there, or is it staged?,'" Kressley told *Daily Variety* journalist Amy Dawes. "Listen, it really is that bad. If you could only smell it." Douglas said he once carved the resident's name in the dirt of a bathtub with a knife, and "one place was so dirty we had to get inhalers," Filicia told *People* writers Allison Adato and Mary Green.

The show's producers try to keep each shopping and renovation budget under $10,000. The Fab Five have noted that it is important to make changes that the man can easily adapt to, and not introduce a high-maintenance new situation. Some of the goodies are thanks to savvy product placement or sponsorship deals. Filicia said that his role on the show is more satisfying in some ways than his work as interior decorator to affluent clients in the New York City area. "In my world, I can spend millions of dollars on somebody's living room, and they'll still ask me why the light switch in the corner by the piano isn't perfectly straight," he told *Entertainment Weekly*'s Nicholas Fonseca. "And now, all of a sudden, these people with a living room full of Pottery Barn objects can't thank me enough."

expert. A Long Island native of Italian and Puerto Rican heritage, he was a talented musical theater star in high school. After college he relocated to New York City, where he landed a role in the hit Broadway musical *Rent,* playing Angel, a drag queen. Rodriguez actually joined *Queer Eye* midway through its second episode, after the producers decided to replace the original culture expert.

## Idea for show came by accident

*Queer Eye*'s beginnings hark back to an incident at a Boston art gallery. Television producer David Collins overheard a woman scolding her husband because of his sloppy clothes. She pointed out a group of well-dressed men and wondered why he couldn't dress more like they did. The men overheard, and came over to offer some friendly tips. After listening to the exchange, Collins dreamed up a television show along the same lines, where five openly gay men would give advice and help to a straight man in need of a makeover.

Each of the five would have an area of expertise, including fashion, grooming, interior design, food and wine, and culture. Collins pitched the idea to cable's Bravo Network, who agreed to it in early 2002. It took nearly a year and a half before the first episode aired. Collins and the show's other executives auditioned several hundred men to find the right mix of experts with the perfect on-screen chemistry. They also had some trouble lining up advertisers, who seemed nervous about the title.

When the first episode of *Queer Eye for the Straight Guy* aired on July 15, 2003, it set a record for the most-watched debut show ever to appear on the Bravo cable channel. Its Tuesday night 10 P.M. time slot went on to set new records each week after that. The show's format is a relatively simple one. The Fab Five surprise their latest victim at his door. They go through his apartment and closet, poking fun at much of it. They come up with an improvement plan on the spot, and take their new "client" shopping. Visits to a hair salon and furniture store are usually required, too. Meanwhile, they keep him out of his home until Filicia and his team have renovated the living quarters.

The "reveal," in reality TV lingo, happens when the man is allowed back into his home to see the results. He is often overwhelmed by the changes, and is clearly thrilled. Kressley has him model some of the new clothes, Allen takes him into the kitchen for a primer on making a special meal, and Douglas sets him up with a new range of men's grooming products. Finally, Rodriguez gives suggestions on how to make a special party or date even more unique. On occasion Rodriguez has even taken his protégé to a workout studio and provided dance lessons. Near the close of the hour-long show, the Fab Five gather in a living room elsewhere and watch what happens when their "made-over" subject's girlfriend, wife, or guests arrive to see the new and improved straight guy.

## The feel-good makeover show

*Queer Eye for the Straight Guy* earned rave reviews. The *New Yorker*'s Nancy Franklin liked the non-threatening way the experts helped each style-challenged subject. "Instead of making him feel ashamed of his bad habits, they storm his domestic prison with humor and set

him free into a new life, giving him the know-how to make him competent and confident," she noted. *Newsweek* writers Devin Gordon and B. J. Sigesmund also liked the show's upbeat approach. "The real secret to the show's success," they noted, was due to the way it set itself apart from other reality TV shows. They wrote that while "programs like 'Extreme Makeover' leave a residue of self-hatred, 'Queer Eye' is surpassingly sweet."

There was also some criticism of *Queer Eye*. A few conservative commentators borrowed U.S. Supreme Court Justice Antonin Scalia (1936–)'s term "culture war" to describe what they viewed as an onslaught of gay-positive images in popular culture. Some in the gay community also disapproved of the show. They worried that the show played into stereotypes about gay men as campy interior decorator or hairdresser types. In the end, however, few had anything genuinely harsh to say about the show and its five new icons. "By playing into gay stereotypes, the Fab 5, paradoxically, lay them to rest," noted the

*The cast of* **Queer Eye for the Straight Guy** *at a book signing in New York City.* © Nancy Kaszerman/Corbis.

*Advocate*'s Bruce C. Steele. "They're so personable and sharp and real that the cliches they embody are magically reconstructed as richly human, without the tiniest swatch of shame."

*Queer Eye* made it onto Bravo's parent company, NBC, for a special half-hour version that drew six million viewers. It spawned a soundtrack and book, and an order for forty new episodes. The Fab Five noted that they were stunned by the popularity of the show, and found it even more amazing that teens were tuning in. Some wrote to express thanks, or thanked them in public. Nearly all of the Fab Five recalled the painful adolescent years before they told friends and family that they were gay. "The toughest part of my life was junior high," Kressley told *Daily Variety* journalist Amy Dawes. "It was really stressful. I used to get threatened. I'd puke in the bathroom at school.... So I thought, I'll just be funny, because when people are laughing, they're not trying to beat you up." That humor found an ideal outlet on television, and Kressley has delivered many of the show's funniest quips. "This place screams women's correctional facility," he once commented after surveying a particularly bleak living room.

Rodriguez, who recorded an album of songs after the first *Queer Eye* season, had a tough time telling his parents that he was gay, partly because they were born-again Christians. It was only when they wanted to come and see his performance in *Rent* that he was able to tell them he was gay. "Our parents work very hard to make our lives charmed, and when there is any deviation from the plan, they worry," he explained in an interview with Minneapolis *Star Tribune* reporter Delma J. Francis. "But because of the show's success and people they know are so accepting of me, they're happy."

Both Kressley and Filicia had once worried that their career choices would upset their parents. Kressley recalled to *Newsweek* writer Marc Peyser that as a child, "I so wanted to be an interior designer or a fashion designer, and it didn't seem like an option because it was too gay, too out there.... I wasted a lot of years." Douglas pointed out that times had changed in the years since they were teenagers, and remarked that each of the Fab Five now had a number of heterosexual male friends not unlike their show's guest stars. "It's very validating to hang out with straight guys and be accepted," Douglas told Michael Giltz in the *Advocate*. "So many of us, we were not accepted when we were younger by straight persons in high school."

# For More Information

## *Periodicals*

Adato, Allison, and Mary Green. "Designing Guy: With a Thriving Home Design Biz and a New Commercial Gig, Thom Filicia Sets His Sights Beyond Queer Eye." *People* (May 3, 2004): p. 99.

Dawes, Amy. "Saving Straight Guys: Couture Crusader Went from Indie Styling to Mainstream." *Daily Variety* (March 26, 2004): p. A8.

Doonan, Simon. "Queer Eye, My Eye! Cast Harasses Hairy Heteros." *New York Observer* (October 27, 2003): p. 31.

Evans, Matthew W. "Queer Eye Guy Aims to Heal." *WWD* (April 23, 2004): p. 8.

Fonseca, Nicholas. "They're Here! They're Queer! And They Don't Like Your End Tables!" *Entertainment Weekly* (August 8, 2003): p. 24.

Francis, Delma J. "Bravo for 'Queer Eye'; 15 Minutes with Thom and Jai." *Star Tribune* (Minneapolis, MN) (March 9, 2004): p. 1E.

Franklin, Nancy. "Keeping Up Appearances. ('Nip/Tuck') (Queer Eye for the Straight Guy)." *New Yorker* (July 28, 2003): p. 92.

"The Gift of Fab: On Bravo's Surprise Hit Queer Eye for the Straight Guy, Five Gay Makeover Maestros Radically Transform Style-Challenged Heteros: Drab Clothes Give Way to DKNY, Messy-Closet Cases Get Tidied, and the Beast Finally Visits the Beauty Salon. Don't forget to 'joozh' that hair!" *People* (August 11, 2003): p. 54.

Giltz, Michael. "Queer Eye Confidential: The Firings! The Budgets! The Filthy Bathtub! Queer Eye for the Straight Guy's Fab 5 and Their Two Equally Fab Producers Spill the Beans on How Reality TV's Queerest Twist Turned into the Hottest Show of the Summer." *Advocate* (September 2, 2003): p. 40.

Gordon, Devin, and B.J. Sigesmund. "Queen for a Day: Bravo's 'Queer Eye for the Straight Guy' Has Exploded. It's a Makeover Takeover." *Newsweek* (August 11, 2003): p. 50.

Hamashige, Hope. "Review of *Music For Every Occasion,* Jai Rodriguez." *People* (March 1, 2004): p. 51.

Kanner, Melinda. "Questions for Queer Eye." *Gay & Lesbian Review Worldwide* (March-April 2004): p. 35.

Larson, Megan. "Bravo Announces Queer Eye Spin-Off During '04 upfront." *Mediaweek* (April 12, 2004): p. 4.

Mullman, Jeremy. "Ted's Fab Journey; Talk About a Makeover: 'Queer Eye' Transforms Chicago Journalist Ted Allen into the Toast of TV Land." *Crain's Chicago Business* (Sept 22, 2003): p. 1.

Paoletta, Michael. "His Eye's Now on His Debut Album." *Record* (Bergen County, NJ) (February 13, 2004): p. 36.

"Pepperidge Farm Hires 'Queer Eye' Star as Spokesman." Knight Ridder/Tribune Business News (April 13, 2004).

Peyser, Marc. "The Fashion Policeman." *Newsweek* (August 11, 2003): p. 51.

"Review: *Queer Eye for the Straight Guy: The Fab 5's Guide to Looking Better, Cooking Better, Dressing Better, Behaving Better, and Living Better.*" *Publishers Weekly* (April 5, 2004): p. 22.

Steele, Bruce C. "The Gay Rights Makeover (Commentary)." *Advocate* (September 2, 2003): p. 40.

Wolfe, Alexandra. "Power Punk: Carson Kressley." *New York Observer* (December 15, 2003): p. 1.

# Daniel Radcliffe

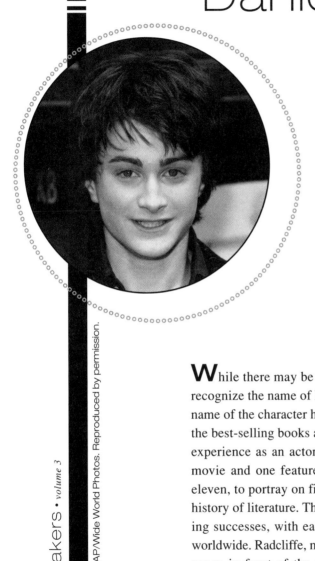

*July 23, 1989  •  London, England*

Actor

**W**hile there may be a number of people in the world who do not recognize the name of Daniel Radcliffe, many millions do know the name of the character he plays: Harry Potter, boy wizard and hero of the best-selling books and blockbuster films. Radcliffe had minimal experience as an actor—he had scored small roles in a television movie and one feature film—when he was chosen, at the age of eleven, to portray on film one of the most popular characters in the history of literature. The *Harry Potter* films have been record-breaking successes, with each earning close to $1 billion at box offices worldwide. Radcliffe, meanwhile, has gone from childhood to adolescence in front of the camera, a transition that has paralleled the increasingly adult situations Harry must confront. While some observers have wondered whether Radcliffe will mature too quickly to be convincing as the young Harry Potter in the final movies of the series, millions of fans cannot imagine any other actor wearing Harry's trademark round glasses and brandishing his magic wand.

## Debut role: monkey

Daniel Jacob Radcliffe was born in London, England, in 1989, less than ten years before the publication of author J. K. Rowling's first *Harry Potter* novel. His parents, Alan Radcliffe and Marcia Gresham, had been involved in the entertainment industry, both having worked as actors at one point. Alan went on to become a literary agent, helping authors get publishing deals, and Marcia became a casting director, helping filmmakers find performers for film and television roles. Alan would later put his own career on hold to manage that of his son. Daniel Radcliffe, an only child, wanted to be an actor from an early age, but his parents would not allow him to audition for professional

> **"**I like playing someone who is a complete underdog. Harry is a huge hero, but he's not perfect. He's completely awkward around girls. He's not a perfect student. He just scrapes by.**"**

roles. He did perform in a school play at age six—cast as a monkey—and enjoyed the experience so much that he continued to ask his parents to let him try out for other shows. When casting began for a film adaptation of nineteenth-century English author Charles Dickens's *Oliver Twist,* Radcliffe renewed his pleadings with his parents. They initially refused to let him audition, concerned that he was too young. By the time they had changed their minds, it was too late—the film had been cast.

Another opportunity arose when, in the late 1990s, a television production based on another classic Dickens novel, *David Copperfield,* was searching for an actor. Radcliffe auditioned for the role of the young David Copperfield, and he won the part, thus beginning his career as a professional actor. The film, which was jointly produced by the British Broadcasting Corporation (BBC) and the Public Broadcasting Service (PBS) in the United States, aired in 1999 and earned positive reviews. Radcliffe's performance was praised, in a review at

## The Other Kids: Ron and Hermione

While not as front-and-center as Harry Potter is, his best pals Ron and Hermione are nonetheless critical elements of the stories. Rupert Grint plays the part of Ron Weasley, Harry's anxiety-ridden redheaded friend. A huge fan of J. K. Rowling's *Harry Potter* books, Grint desperately wanted to be chosen to portray Ron when casting began for the first film. He felt they shared much in common: both have red hair and come from big families; both love sweets and are terrified of spiders. His passion paid off when Grint was selected from among thousands of boys to play the part.

Grint was born August 24, 1988, in the small English town of Hertfordshire. He is the eldest of five children and, when not filming, attends an all-boys school. He loves studying science and playing sports and videogames. For his fourteenth birthday, Grint asked for and received a unicycle. He has told reporters that he loves making films and would like to continue in the role of Ron for as long as possible. As for life beyond *Harry Potter,* Grint speculated in an article in *People* magazine: "When I was a kid I wanted to be an ice-cream man. That still seems like a cool job."

While she shares Hermione Granger's tendency to be a bit bossy as well as her self-confidence and intense loyalty to friends, Emma Watson also points out that there are many ways in which she departs from the character she portrays. She performs well in school but is not nearly as academically disciplined as her on-screen counterpart. Watson's friends are mostly girls, unlike Hermione's, and she spends her free time hanging out with friends, playing such sports as field hockey and rounders (similar to American softball). Watson pointed out another difference in an interview with *Time for Kids:* "I am also much more obsessed with clothes and shopping whereas Hermione has no fashion sense at all."

Born April 13, 1990, Watson lives in Oxford, England, home of the famed Oxford University. Before auditioning for the role of Hermione, she had acted in several school plays but had not performed professionally. Just as her costars did, Watson beat out thousands of other hopefuls trying out for her role. She loves the camaraderie on the set, joining in with her costars to play pranks on the other actors. In an article for the Asia Africa Intelligence Wire, Watson insisted that her life has not changed dramatically since winning the part of Hermione: "I mean, obviously I'm recognized on the way from home a lot more and, let's face it, I have an action figure of myself. But apart from that I'm just trying to keep my life as normal as possible."

the Web site *culturevulture.net,* for being believable and down-to-earth: "Daniel Radcliffe has a naturalistic presence—rare enough in child actors—and he seems like a real boy." Radcliffe later earned a small role in the feature film *The Tailor of Panama* (2001), portraying the son of characters played by Geoffrey Rush (1951–) and Jamie Lee Curtis (1958–). Starring Pierce Brosnan (1953–) and directed by John Boorman, the film—which was based on a book by esteemed spy novelist John LeCarré—was modestly successful at the box office and earned the admiration of a number of reviewers.

When Curtis, Radcliffe's costar and screen mom in *The Tailor of Panama,* initially met the young actor, she made a connection between him and the ultrapopular character Harry Potter, immediately imagining Radcliffe portraying the boy wizard in the yet-to-be-made first film. She told *Entertainment Weekly* in 2000: "The first time I laid eyes on this kid, I said, 'He's Harry Potter. He should be Harry Potter.' He's the perfect choice." The man chosen to direct that upcoming film, Chris Columbus, also had his eye on Radcliffe, having seen the boy's performance in *David Copperfield.* Concerned about the intensity of attention their son would certainly receive if he portrayed Harry Potter, Radcliffe's parents at first declined. Then one evening the Radcliffes, accompanied by their son, ran into their friend David Heyman at the theater. Heyman was sitting with Steve Kloves, the writer who had written the screenplay for the first *Harry Potter* film. Radcliffe could not help but notice that the two men repeatedly turned around to look at him during the performance. Heyman, who also happened to be the film's producer, took one look at Daniel Radcliffe and felt the long search for an actor to portray Harry Potter was over. "Right then," Heyman told Terry Lawson of Knight Ridder/Tribune News Service, "I knew I had found our Harry." He spoke to the Radcliffes about his feelings, and they eventually reconsidered, allowing Daniel to try out for the role. In spite of the director and producer's hunch about Radcliffe being right for the role, the actor still had to go through three rounds of auditions before being cast. Radcliffe was taking a bath one evening when his father told him he had won the role. "I cried," he recalled to Stephen Schaefer of the *Boston Globe.* "It was so cool."

## Instant fame

Radcliffe went overnight from being a boy who dabbled in acting to the instantly famous actor who would embody Harry Potter in a highly anticipated film adaptation. The first Harry Potter novel, *Harry Potter and the Sorcerer's Stone* (titled *Harry Potter and the Philosopher's Stone* in England and Canada), had made a literary superstar of author J. K. Rowling. Millions of fans all over the globe were ready to shower their intense Potter devotion to the film—or to condemn it to obscurity if it betrayed the spirit of the beloved novel. To the relief of the book's fans, Rowling was involved in the film's casting and other aspects of production. As reported by Dana Harris in *Variety,* the author gave Radcliffe her seal of approval: "Having seen Dan Radcliffe's screen test, I don't think Chris Columbus could have found a better Harry." In the midst of his newfound celebrity, Radcliffe began shooting the first film, joined by a cast of notable English actors and fellow novices Rupert Grint and Emma Watson portraying Harry's best pals Ron and Hermione.

Released in November of 2001, the first film in the series scored a huge success at the box office, earning close to $1 billion worldwide. The movie chronicles Harry Potter's journey from his unhappy life with an emotionally abusive aunt and uncle to his enchanted existence as a young wizard learning his trade at the Hogwarts School of Witchcraft and Wizardry. Thrilled at the prospect of seeing Rowling's vividly described world come to life on the big screen, millions of fans in countries all over the world flocked to theaters. Some fans, and many critics, left theaters somewhat disappointed, complaining that the film was competent and faithful to the book but lacked sparkle and imagination. Mindful of the importance of staying true to the much-loved book, the filmmakers had tread carefully, creating a film that many described as a slavish imitation. *Time* magazine's Richard Corliss expressed the feelings of several reviewers when he wrote, "The film lacks moviemaking buoyancy—the feeling of soaring in space that Rowling's magic-carpet prose gives the reader." Even many who found the film lacking approved of the casting and praised the actors' performances, including *Newsweek*'s David Ansen: "His eyes dancing with intelligence, Daniel Radcliffe is a mercifully unsentimental Harry Potter, likable and inquisitive but slightly aloof, his self-possession the necessary defense of an orphan raised by hostile Muggles [non-magical humans]."

The second chapter in the projected seven-film series, *Harry Potter and the Chamber of Secrets,* was released one year later, in November of 2002. Again approaching the $1 billion mark in global box-office tallies, the film intensified Pottermania while drawing some of the same criticism that had been aimed at the first. Some reviewers praised the actors and filmmakers for what they perceived as an increased confidence and adventurousness in the second film. Roger Ebert, of the *Chicago Sun-Times,* described the film as "visually alive," concluding his review with the exclamation, "What a glorious movie."

Others, however, felt that for all its faithfulness to the original work, this film failed to capture the wonder and glory of Rowling's book. The *San Francisco Chronicle*'s Mick LaSalle wrote: "It's still possible, at times, to tell that *Chamber of Secrets* has, at its foundation, a work of extraordinary imagination and spiritual generosity. But just as often the film is as monotonous and despair-inducing as three hours on an airplane with nothing to read but the in-flight magazine." Regardless of any negative reviews, *Chamber of Secrets* increased the media and fan frenzy surrounding Radcliffe. Even as he was recognized and approached by fans more and more often, however, the young actor tried hard to continue his normal life, getting together with friends and attending school whenever he wasn't filming.

*Richard Harris (left) as Dumble-dore and Daniel Radcliffe in a scene from* **Harry Potter and the Chamber of Secrets.** © The Kobal Collection.

## Time to change

A year and a half after the release of *Chamber of Secrets,* the third installment of the film series was released, and *Harry Potter and the Prisoner of Azkaban* signalled a number of significant changes. A new director, Alfonso Cuaron, had taken over, replacing Columbus, who needed a break after the intense workload of the first two films. Cuaron had achieved fame—and won an Academy Award—for his racy Mexican coming-of-age film *Y Tu Mamà Tambièn* (2001), but he won the *Harry Potter* job in part because of his direction of the film *A Little Princess,* a 1995 children's film that happened to be one of Rowling's favorites. While Radcliffe, Grint, and Watson were initially devastated by Columbus's departure from the series, they eventually embraced Cuaron and credited him with expanding their acting abilities. Cuaron began his acquaintance with the young actors by asking them to write an essay about their characters, prompting them to think about their characters' personality and motivation in ways they had not done with the first two films.

Other major changes involved Radcliffe and his fellow "child" actors, all of whom had grown up considerably during the time between *Chamber of Secrets* and *Prisoner of Azkaban.* In spite of the filmmakers' best efforts to complete the films quickly, the young actors were maturing faster than the characters, causing tremendous speculation about whether they would be able to continue in their roles for all seven films. For the time being, however, the actors' plunge into adolescence suited the darker material in *Prisoner of Azkaban,* which brings to the fore the sense of frustration and isolation felt by so many during the transition from childhood to adulthood. In *Prisoner of Azkaban,* Harry is forced to confront complex and sometimes unpleasant realities—about himself, his parents' murders, and the possible betrayal of his parents by their friend Sirius Black. Radcliffe explained to Jeff Jensen of *Entertainment Weekly* that his deep discussions with Cuaron about Harry's emotional state helped him immeasurably. "I'll forever be in his debt," Radcliffe told Jensen. "It [Cuaron's guidance] basically affected the way I approached everything after that."

The series' new direction earned a higher degree of praise from critics and continued to draw in record-breaking crowds at theaters around the world. Opening on June 4, 2004, *Prisoner of Azkaban* earned nearly $100 million in its first weekend alone. Radcliffe's fame continued to swell, with his every move making headlines. The press wrote that he had surpassed singer Charlotte Church to become the second wealthiest teenager in Britain, behind Prince Harry, grandson of the queen of England. Asked by the *Cincinnati Post* how it feels to grow up in the public eye, Radcliffe shared his strategy for retaining normalcy: "I never read the articles or read what people are saying about me on the Internet. If you read all that you just become so self-conscious." Instead of fretting about the lack of privacy that accompanies fame, Radcliffe focuses on the benefits of his association with Harry Potter. He has had the opportunity to meet and work with many actors he admires, he learned from *Prisoner of Azkaban* costar Gary Oldman (1958–) how to play the bass guitar, and his grades have actually improved since he became a film star. He has developed a passion for movies and thinks about one day becoming a writer or director. Cuaron speculated to Jensen that Radcliffe would grow up to be either an actor, a director, or a rock star. When asked which career he thought he might choose, Radcliffe displayed the self-confidence he has acquired in recent years, querying, "Can't I be all three?"

## For More Information

### Periodicals

Ansen, David. "The Trouble with Harry." *Newsweek* (November 19, 2001): p. 70.

"A Conversation with … Daniel Radcliffe." *Cincinnati Post* (June 5, 2004).

Corliss, Richard. "Wizardry without Magic." *Time* (November 19, 2001): p. 136.

De Vera, Ruel S. "On the Magic Broomstick of Fame, *Harry Potter* Kids Keep Feet on the Ground." Asia Africa Intelligence Wire (November 10, 2002).

Ebert, Roger. "*Harry Potter and the Chamber of Secrets.*" *Chicago Sun-Times* (November 15, 2002).

Fierman, Daniel. "Casting a Spell." *Entertainment Weekly* (September 1, 2000): p. 16.

Harris, Dana. "*Potter* Waves Wand over Brit." *Variety* (August 28, 2000): p. 10.

"Hogwarts 2004." *People* (June 14, 2004): p. 126.

Jensen, Jeff. "Lucky Thirteen?" *Entertainment Weekly* (June 11, 2004): p. 32.

LaSalle, Mick. "Tortured *Chamber.*" *San Francisco Chronicle* (November 15, 2002).

Lawson, Terry. "Young Actor Daniel Radcliffe Takes His Starring Role in Stride." Knight Ridder/Tribune News Service (November 14, 2001).

Schaefer, Stephen. "*Harry* Comes, Ready or Not." *Boston Globe* (November 8, 2001).

"TFK Q&A." *Time for Kids* (May 7, 2004): p. 8.

### Web Sites

*The Official Harry Potter Website.* http://harrypotter.warnerbros.co.uk/
main/homepage/home.html (accessed on August 12, 2004).

Wake, Bob. *"David Copperfield." culturevulture.net.* http://www.culture
vulture.net/Television/DavidCopperfield.htm (accessed on August 11,
2004).

# Michael Ramsay and James Barton

## Michael Ramsay
### c. 1950 • Scotland
### Company executive

## James Barton
### c. 1958 • United States
### Company executive

**M**ichael Ramsay and Jim Barton are the founders of TiVo, the company that makes the revolutionary digital video recorder (DVR) for television. Ramsay and Barton fought tough battles with competitors and other opponents during their first decade in business. TiVo, meanwhile, gained a cult following among users. Some called it the next frontier in television viewing because of the freedom it allowed viewers.

TiVo's founders met when both were top executives at Silicon Graphics, Inc. (SGI). The Mountain View, California-based company was an early pioneer in the development of computer workstations. These were desktop machines with immense computing power. In the early 1990s SGI also became a leader in developing the software used in producing special effects for movies. The dinosaurs in *Jurassic Park* and the tornadoes in *Twister* were two of its biggest successes.

## Silicon Valley success stories

Michael Ramsay was born in Scotland, in the early 1950s. He grew up in Sighthill, a poor section of Edinburgh. After earning a degree in electrical engineering at the University of Edinburgh, he moved to California around 1976. He first worked for computer maker Hewlett-Packard and another company called Convergent Technologies. Both were located in the so-called "Silicon Valley" hub of high-tech businesses near the California cities of San Jose and Palo Alto. SGI became one of Silicon Valley's biggest success stories during the 1980s, and Ramsay rose to become senior vice president and general manager of its visual systems group. He was later involved with

> **"TiVo is the first and only post-Internet Big Idea."**
>
> **Michael Ramsay, *Fortune*, March 19, 2001.**

another division in the company called Silicon Studio, which created interactive digital media applications.

Jim Barton also studied electrical engineering during his undergraduate days. His degree was from the University of Colorado at Boulder, where he earned an advanced degree in computer science. His first jobs were with Bell Laboratories and Hewlett-Packard. At SGI he served as vice president and general manager of the systems software division.

TiVo's roots date back to an infamous failure of the mid-1990s. Ramsay and Barton had both been involved in SGI's work on an exciting new cable television experiment in Orlando, Florida. SGI worked with Time-Warner Cable to help create a two-way cable television system called Full Service Network. It offered four thousand Orlando households some five hundred television channels and a new kind of remote control that allowed viewers to program their favorites. It even took users to a site where they could order a pizza delivery with the click of a button. But the much-hyped Full Service Network never caught on, and reportedly cost Time-Warner $100 million. It was touted as the next generation of online access, but the World Wide

Web took off in earnest in 1995, and users discovered they would rather surf the Web from their desktop computers than from their television screens.

Barton served as the lead system software architect for the Full Service Interactive software, but moved on to a project between SGI and AT&T Network Systems. This was called Interactive Digital Solutions Company, and Barton was its chief technology officer. He eventually left the company and founded Network Age Software, becoming its president and chief executive officer.

## Dreamed of futuristic "home network"

Ramsay and Barton joined forces after Ramsay left SGI in May of 1997. Because of their combined work history, it was easy for them to get appointments with venture capital firms in Silicon Valley. These investment companies provided start-up money to new businesses in exchange for a stake in future profits. With a venture capital check for $3 million in the bank to start their own company, they began brainstorming ideas for consumer products. They first tried to come up with a way to connect appliances in a home with a computer and Internet access. In their "home networking" vision, a sensor in the refrigerator could tell when a carton of milk was going bad, and automatically order a fresh delivery to the home from a grocery service. A resident would be able to turn his thermostat up or down from his home office chair. But Ramsay and Barton realized the idea presented too many potential roadblocks. As they later told *New York Times Magazine* writer Michael Lewis, "When you build a company around a technology and someone says, 'Tell me again what this thing does?' you need to be able to say, 'It does this.' We found that we couldn't say what home networking did."

Ramsay and Barton had come up with the company name "Teleworld," and kept that name when they changed their vision to that of working solely with the most-used home appliance—the television. Their idea was a "personal television receiver." It would use a digital chip to give television viewers a ground-breaking degree of control over what they watched and when they watched it. The personal television receiver sat on top of the television, much like a VCR or cable box, and was linked to the outside world via a telephone line. They came up with a quirky brand name, "TiVo," and an animated logo.

They asked the venture capital firms for another $300 million, and used the money to launch their company in earnest.

Although the TiVo box looked a little like a VCR, it was much easier to program. It could store up to forty hours of programming if instructed, and had an innovative "Season Pass" feature. The Season Pass would record an entire season's worth of a series with just one or two clicks of the remote. A TiVo user could then watch what had been recorded, with the ability to fast-forward through commercials. TiVo also let viewers pause during a live program. TiVo contained a unique "smart" feature that could tape shows based on what a user had previously recorded. As Lewis wrote in the *New York Times Magazine* article, the company now had a clear idea to sell to investors: "When someone asked Barton or Ramsay, 'Tell me again what this gadget does?' they now had a simple answer: 'It lets you watch anything you want to watch when you want to watch it.'"

## Company struggled in early years

The first TiVos were introduced in the United States in early 1999. They sold for about $500 each. Buyers also committed to a $9.95 monthly subscription fee to use TiVo's unique features. An initial public offering of stock by the new company later in 1999 was a great success. There was tremendous early buzz about TiVo, along with rumors that it would forever change the public's viewing habits. Still, the company struggled for the next few years, and posted huge financial losses. Some of those losses came because it sold the digital video recorder, called a "DVR," below cost in order to lure new users. Still, TiVo was slow to catch on with consumers. By the end of 2000, it was in just 150,000 U.S. households. The company also made a mistake with some of its first advertising campaigns, one of which cost $50 million. That first generation of TiVo television commercials, marketing experts claimed, did not explain the innovative new technology well enough.

Despite the early financial worries, many saw the potential in Ramsay and Barton's idea. The partners struck deals with America Online (AOL), DirecTV, Comcast, and Walt Disney. "TiVo's courtship of investors … was impressive," wrote *Fortune*'s Christine Y. Chen. "By venture capital standards, it wasn't exactly a big draw.

The company had an expensive business model and was creating a new consumer electronics category. It was subsidizing its hardware, was service- and subscription-oriented, and was unlikely to become profitable for years. But Ramsay and Barton's vision for customized television ultimately proved too strong to resist."

Ramsay and Barton decided to stop spending money on big advertising campaigns and let TiVo take hold through word of mouth instead. In time, a minor cult of enthusiastic TiVo users sprang up, and articles on the new programming device began to fuel the public interest. One such article was a 2000 *New York Times Magazine* cover story by Michael Lewis. The writer compared the importance of the date that TiVo was founded, August 4, 1997, to that of November 10, 1994, the founding date of online retailer Amazon.com. And Lewis further argued that TiVo had the potential to forever change commercial television broadcasting. As Ramsay told Lewis, "One question our investors did ask us is 'How long will it take for the TV networks to hate you so much that they shut you down?'"

## TiVo affects advertising

Ramsay and Barton met several other challenges over the next half-decade. There was competition with Replay TV, a rival. There were also patent violation lawsuits. But as TiVo began to catch on, television networks did indeed become fearful that the end was near. Major broadcast networks like CBS and Fox were able to sell advertising slots for *Survivor, American Idol,* and other top-rated TV shows for millions of dollars per minute. And TiVo users were said to especially love the ability to skip over commercials. But Ramsay and Barton pointed out that TiVo actually offered new potential markets for media companies and advertisers: TiVo could collect data on viewers and offer it for sale to marketing companies. It also launched a new "showcase" feature, where a viewer could click a button on the remote control and request more information on an advertised product.

Ramsay gave up one of his job titles when TiVo hired longtime NBC executive Marty Yudkowitz to guide the company as its new president. Ramsay became board chair and chief executive officer, while Barton served as TiVo's chief technology officer. The company reached its one-millionth subscriber mark in November of 2003. But it was also facing renewed competition from Microsoft, Sony, and even hackers posting how-to guides on how to triple the memory space in the boxes on a do-it-yourself basis.

Ramsay and Barton hoped that TiVo would be in thirty million households by 2007. In the spring of 2004 they announced a new venture that would allow TiVo users to download movies and music from the Internet. But their original idea has become so common that "TiVo" even began to be used as a verb. Barton's favorite shows to "TiVo" are *Star Trek* reruns and Comedy Central's *The Daily Show.* One of Ramsay's favorite shows is the real-time thriller *24.* Journalist Frank Rose in *Wired,* compared Ramsay to the hero of that very series, played by Kiefer Sutherland. "Like Jack Bauer," wrote Rose, Ramsay "pinballs from one crisis to another as powerful enemies, shifting alliances, and relentless plot twists conspire to do him in. The specter of betrayal lurks behind every encounter. The clock is ticking. Any minute his bigger, better-financed adversaries—major cable carriers, PC and consumer electronics giants—will arrive on the scene to blow him away."

## For More Information

*Periodicals*

Bevens, Nick. "Times Are Changing as TiVo Looks to Kill the Video." *Evening News* (Edinburgh, Scotland) (August 22, 2001): p. B4.

Carnoy, David. "Anthony Wood and Mike Ramsay Are at War." *Success* (March 1999): p. 52.

Chen, Christine Y. "TiVo Is Smart TV (But Hey, Brains Aren't Everything.)." *Fortune* (March 19, 2001): p. 124.

Coppa, Matt. "The Tao of TiVo: Wisdom from the Men Who Changed How the World Watches TV." *Men's Fitness* (May 2004): p. 78.

Einstein, David. "SGI Reorganizes, 2 Execs Depart." *San Francisco Chronicle* (May 6, 1997): p. C1.

"Here's the Next 'Next Big Thing.'" *Business Week* (August 9, 1999): p. 38.

"Is TiVo's Signal Fading?" *Business Week* (September 10, 2001): p. 72.

Lewis, Michael. "Boom Box." *New York Times Magazine* (August 13, 2000): p. 36.

Markoff, John. "New Service by TiVo Will Build Bridges From Internet to the TV." *New York Times* (June 9, 2004).

McHugh, Josh. "TiVo's Turning Point: It Redefined Television. Now Comes Competition." *Wired* (October 2003).

Pitta, Julie. "Interactivity: The Great White Whale." *Forbes* (September 21, 1998): p. 60.

Rose, Frank. "The Fast-Forward, On-Demand, Network-Smashing Future of Television." *Wired* (October 2003).

St. John, Warren. "Friend Or Foe? The Cult of TiVo Cometh." *New York Times* (April 20, 2003): p. 1.

Taub, Eric A. "How Do I Love Thee, TiVo?" *New York Times* (March 18, 2004): p. G1.

Turner, Nick. "If TiVo Succeeds, Will It Attract Many Suitors?" *Investor's Business Daily* (January 3, 2002): p. A6.

Woolley, Scott. "Zap!" *Forbes* (September 29, 2003): p. 76.

### *Web Sites*

"Management Team: Jim Barton." *TiVo.com.* http://www.tivo.com/5.2.3.asp (accessed on June 1, 2004).

"Management Team: Michael Ramsay." *TiVo.com.* http://www.tivo.com/5.2.1.asp (accessed on June 1, 2004).

Stone, Brad. "TiVo's Big Moment." *MSNBC.* http://www.msnbc.msn.com/id/4208945/ (accessed on June 1, 2004).

# Raven

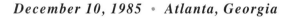

Chris Weeks/Wire Image.com.

*December 10, 1985* • *Atlanta, Georgia*

## Actress

**T**een actress Raven stars in the hit Disney Channel series *That's So Raven*. Many fans of her show, however, may not be old enough to recognize Raven from her first television role. In the early 1990s Raven charmed audiences as the youngest member of the Huxtable clan on the last few seasons of the top-rated NBC sitcom *The Cosby Show*. At the time, she was known by the stage name Raven-Symoné, which she later shortened.

## Starred in television commercials

Raven was born Raven-Symoné Christina Pearman in Atlanta, Georgia, on December 10, 1985. Her parents, Christopher and Lydia Pearman, believed their infant daughter had star power at an early age, and she landed a modeling contract before her second birthday. Soon the family relocated to New York City to boost her chances. There the toddler appeared in television commercials for products such as Cool

Whip and Ritz Crackers, among others. Her talents led to an audition for a part in a Bill Cosby (1937–) film called *Ghost Dad,* but she did not win the role.

The audition, however, impressed Cosby, a veteran actor and comedian. Since 1984 he had headed the cast of the *The Cosby Show,* the hit NBC series that was said to have revived the sitcom format. In it, Cosby played Heathcliff Huxtable, a likable physician. "Cliff" was married to a no-nonsense attorney, Clair, played by Phylicia Rashad (1948–), and they had five children. The Huxtable kids ranged from college student Sondra, played by Sabrina LeBeauf, to pre-schooler Rudy, played by Keshia Knight Pulliam (1979–).

> **"I just want to represent my people well. I'm not going to be ghetto on the show. I don't want people to think that's all we can do."**

Even at a young age, Raven was familiar with *The Cosby Show.* As her father told *Ebony* journalist Douglas C. Lyons, Raven liked to watch little Knight Pulliam's Rudy character, and "would always say, 'I can do that. Why can't I be on The Cosby Show?'" Her chance came in 1989, when the second Huxtable daughter, played by Lisa Bonet (1967–), returned to the show. Bonet had left to star in a spin-off, set at college, called *A Different World.* She left both series for a time, and her return to *Cosby* came as the newly married Denise Huxtable. Denise's husband was a single parent and Navy officer who was often away at sea, and Denise returned to her parents' Brooklyn brownstone home with her husband's toddler daughter, Olivia Kendall, played by Raven.

## Found steady work

Raven was an immediate hit as *Cosby*'s newest cast member. She soon became a celebrity at the young age of five. She recalled being thrilled the first time a fan requested an autograph. "And I signed my whole name right," she boasted to Lyons. She played Olivia for the

## The *Cosby* Phenomenon

The *Cosby Show* was a major television event of the 1984 season. From its debut, the show's mix of comedy and gentle moral lessons appealed to audiences of all colors. Critics called it the show that helped renew faith in the half-hour situation comedy on network television. The Cosby household included eldest daughter Sondra, who was often away at college; Denise, the fashionably dressed teen rebel; Theo, the sole son and a prankster; drama-queen Vanessa; and Rudy, an adorable kindergartner.

With popular comedian Bill Cosby cast as a New York City obstetrician with an attorney wife, *Cosby* was said to be the first television series to show a black middle-class family. But their skin color, others noted, was beside the point. The Huxtables' problems were similar to those of any family. Cliff and Clair struggled to make sure their children understood the importance of their education. They dealt with the occasional discipline problem firmly and with a sense of humor. The series, noted *Time* critic Richard Zoglin, "initiated a healthy new attitude toward race on TV by building a show around an upper-middle-class family that just happened to be black. And it set a standard for wholesome TV families that inspired backlash (*Married … with Children*) as well as imitation (*Family Matters*)."

The *Cosby Show* held the number-one spot in television ratings for four years in the late 1980s. It was the most successful sitcom of the decade, and won an Emmy Award for Outstanding Comedy Series. Raven joined the show as it was nearing the end of its run. She debuted on it in 1989 as Olivia Kendall, stepdaughter to a newly married Denise. She seemed cast to fill the "cute" slot occupied earlier by Keshia Knight Pulliam's Rudy, and she did so admirably for the final three seasons, trading lines with Cosby's Cliff Huxtable and winning some of the biggest laughs in each episode. But as the other Huxtable children grew into their teens and adulthood, the show's writers struggled to keep its plots fresh. It began losing ratings to a new series from the Fox Network, *The Simpsons,* and its final episode aired in the spring of 1992.

Raven's little Olivia lives on in reruns of *The Cosby Show*. She occasionally catches glimpses of herself as a scene-stealing five-year-old, but finds it to be a strange experience. "It's funny, when I watch the show I don't think of Olivia as being me," Raven told *WWD* writer Julee Greenberg. "I sort of think of her as someone else, since I was too young to remember so much of it."

final three seasons on *Cosby,* which ended its run in 1992. In 1993 she landed a role in another top sitcom, *Hangin' With Mr. Cooper,* playing the part of Nicole Lee. She also made her feature film debut in 1994 in a remake of *The Little Rascals.* A bigger movie role came in 1998 when she appeared as Eddie Murphy (1961–)'s daughter in the box office hit *Dr. Dolittle,* and she also appeared in its 2001 sequel.

During the 1990s Raven divided her time between school and show business. Child labor laws required her to have a tutor if her television and movie parts were being shot during the months when school was in session. She also went into the recording studio, and her debut album, *Here's To New Dreams,* was released in 1993, the same year she turned eight. She had reportedly been the youngest solo artist ever signed to the MCA label. She was a teenager by the time her second album of pop and R&B tunes, *Undeniable,* appeared in 1999.

Raven was hired by Disney as she neared the end of her high school years at Atlanta's North Springs High. She was originally cast in a supporting role on a new show called *Absolutely Psychic,* but executives were impressed by her talent and decided to rework the script with her in the lead. *That's So Raven* debuted on the Disney Channel in January of 2003, and from the start proved to be a hit with viewers in the nine-to-fourteen age group. Raven plays Raven Baxter, a San Francisco high school student who struggles with her psychic abilities. Only her two best friends and her parents know about her secret gift. Raven's character is a likable, normal teenager who is a bit of a klutz, but "her visions give her a real mysteriousness," the actress told Suzanne Mac-Neille in an article in the *New York Times.* Raven explained, "They are the one thing that makes her humble." She added that her character tries to keep her special talent from intruding on her normal teenage life. "Raven doesn't want just anyone to know about her visions," she told MacNeille. "She's afraid people will think she's a freak."

*Raven signs autographs at the premiere of* Cheetah Girls, *in New York City.* AP/Wide World Photo. Reproduced by permission.

## Newest "tween" star

Though the veteran teen actress no longer had to make a special effort to spell her entire name correctly for autographs, she was in turn amused by her young fans. "Little kids are coming up to me asking me 'What's my future?'" she told *Jet* "'I'm not really psychic,'" she explained to them, as she told the magazine. "And they are like, 'No, what's my future?' And I am like, 'OK, you are going to have a good future.'"

Raven was hailed as a member of the new "tween" actor category, and as the Disney Channel's next big star. There were many comparisons to *Lizzie McGuire,* the Disney hit that propelled Hilary Duff (1987–) to fame. Nicholas Fonseca in *Entertainment Weekly* declared that Raven's "quick rise may herald a new era at the network, one with a curvy, sassy black girl as its poster child." Like Duff, Raven also began appearing in other Disney projects. She was cast in the lead in *The Cheetah Girls,* a cable movie that aired in the summer of 2003. It won the highest rating for a cable show that week, with more than six million viewers tuning in. *The Cheetah Girls* was based on a series of young adult novels, and Raven starred as Galleria Garibaldi, an ambitious New York City high school student who leads a singing group of three friends. In the movie the girls head for stardom in the midst of drama, excitement, and a lot of animal-print fashion. Laura Fries, writing in *Daily Variety,* gave the show a mixed review: "Ironically, 'Cheetah Girls' supposedly denounces manufactured pop music and marketing over artistry, yet it plays like a two-hour fashion commercial and culminates in a ridiculous lip-synching extravaganza." Yet Fries also noted that the cable movie "does have a few things going for it, namely Raven, an appealing and versatile young actress who has charm and skill."

*The Cheetah Girls* seemed good preparation for Raven to appear as the lead in upcoming Hollywood movies. She was cast in *Sparkle,* a remake of a 1976 musical film about three sisters who form a girl group. The original starred a young Irene Cara (1959–), who later appeared in the hit movie *Fame.* Raven would take the Cara role as the youngest Sparkle sister. It was a part once planned for Aaliyah (1979–2001), before her untimely death in a plane crash. Raven was also slated to star in *All-American Girl,* a 2004 movie based on a book by Meg Cabot (1967–), the author of *The Princess Diaries.* In it, she is cast as a teenager who inadvertently saves the U.S. president's life. There is also a third pop album in the works.

## "I'm not your normal girl"

Raven has always remembered the advice that veteran actor Bill Cosby gave her: "'Stay professional and always stay sweet,'" she recalled to an interviewer for *Jet.* She had a difficult time in one scene during her first season of *That's So Raven,* she told the *New York Times.* The script called for her to let a boa constrictor snake be wrapped around her neck. She was so frightened of the reptile that she began crying, and "the sick faces I'm making are for real," she confessed to MacNeille.

Raven eventually moved out of her parents' home to share a place with another tween star, Lindsay Lohan (1986–). They live in Los Angeles, where Raven's Disney series is taped. A food lover, she has said that she would like to attend culinary school some day, if her schedule permits. She admits that her figure is curvier than normal for actresses on television and in films. "I'm not your normal girl that you see on television," she told *Palm Beach Post* writer Kevin D. Thompson. "I'm not 95 pounds.… But when you look at the movies and you look at all the girls who are hot now, I wonder if I could've been in those movies if I was skinny." She also discussed her figure in an interview with *WWD*'s Julee Greenberg. Raven said she has considered offers to launch her own makeup or apparel line, but "if I was to do my own clothing line, I would do it for girls who are built like me," she told Greenberg. "When I shop for myself it's very hard to find clothes. I'm curvy and there should be more clothes out there for curvy girls."

## For More Information

### Periodicals

Fleming, Michael. "Raven Flocks to Pic: Young Thesp to 'Sparkle' in Thrush Tale Redo." *Daily Variety* (August 18, 2003): p. 5.

Fonseca, Nicholas. "The New Tween Queen: Former Cosby Show-Stealer and Current Disney Channel Icon Raven is So Not Lizzie McGuire." *Entertainment Weekly* (October 17, 2003): p. 42.

Fries, Laura. "The Cheetah Girls. (Movie Review.)" *Daily Variety* (August 15, 2003): p. 8.

Greenberg, Julee. "Quotes From Raven; With 'The Cosby Show' Behind Her Raven Prepares to Be a Cheetah Girl." *WWD* (August 7, 2003): p. 12.

Lipton, Michael A. "Cos and Effect: All Grown Up, the Cosby Show Kids Recall the Landmark Show That Celebrated a New Kind of TV Family." *People* (May 20, 2002): p. 140.

Lyons, Douglas C. "Show Biz Kids: Pre-Teen Stars Find That Success in the Spotlight Is Not All Fun and Child's Play." *Ebony* (May 1990): p. 106.

MacNeille, Suzanne. "Visions of Peril Dance in Her Head (But It's a Secret)." *New York Times* (January 12, 2003): p. 59.

Moses, Michael. "Raven." *Teen People* (February 1, 2004): p. 93.

"Raven Cute 'Cosby' Kid Turns Sassy TV Starlet at 17." *Jet* (September 8, 2003): p. 60.

"Raven-Symone Releases Her Debut Pop Album." *Jet* (July 5, 1993): p. 61.

Thompson, Kevin D. "Raven Wonders If 'Thicky-Thick' a Liability." *Palm Beach Post* (July 13, 2003): p. 5J.

Wright, Heather Keets. "Raven Wins Raves: This Former Cosby Show Cutie Is Now a Disney Diva with Her Own Sitcom!" *Essence* (October 2003): p. 148.

Zoglin, Richard. "The Cosby Show." *Time* (May 4, 1992): p. 76.

# Condoleezza Rice

*November 14, 1954 • Birmingham, Alabama*

## National security adviser

**C**ondoleezza Rice became one of the most influential women in the world of global politics when President George W. Bush (1946–) named her as his national security adviser in December of 2000. Her role became extremely important after the September 11, 2001, attacks on New York City and the Pentagon in Washington. Rice has played a crucial part in shaping the most aggressive U.S. foreign policy in modern history, with wars launched against Afghanistan and Iraq during her time in office.

## Became kindergarten piano prodigy

Rice grew up during a deeply segregated era of American history. She was born in 1954 in Birmingham, Alabama, to parents who were both educators. Her father, John Wesley Rice Jr., was a football coach and high school guidance counselor at one of Birmingham's black public schools. He was also an ordained Presbyterian minister in Birmingham's Westminster Presbyterian Church, which had been founded by his own father, also a minister. Rice's mother, Angelena, was a teacher and church organist. Angelena loved opera, and so named her only child after an Italian-language term, *con dolcezza*. It is used in musical notation and means "to play with sweetness."

Birmingham was clearly divided into black and white spheres during Rice's childhood, and the two worlds rarely met. But her parents were determined that their only child would grow up to be an accomplished and well-rounded young woman. Rice began piano lessons at the age of three, and gave her first recital a year later. She became somewhat of a musical prodigy in the Birmingham area,

**"I find football so interesting strategically. It's the closest thing to war. What you're really doing is taking and yielding territory, and you have certain strategies and tactics."**

performing often at school and community events. In addition to long hours spent practicing the piano, she also took French and Spanish lessons after school, and later became a competitive figure skater. "My whole community was determined not to let their children's horizons be limited by growing up in segregated Birmingham," Rice recalled in an interview with television personality Oprah Winfrey (1954–) for *O, The Oprah Magazine*. "Sometimes I think they overcompensated because they wanted their kids to be so much better."

Not surprisingly, Rice earned good grades in school, even at an early age. Attending segregated schools in Birmingham, she skipped the first grade entirely and was later promoted from the sixth directly into the eighth grade. Her city became a battleground during the emerging civil rights movement in the late 1950s, and the strife directly touched Rice's early life. In 1963 the Sixteenth Street Baptist Church, situated in the middle of Birmingham's black community, was

## "The Most Powerful Woman in the World"

U.S. national security adviser Condoleezza Rice has sometimes been described as the most influential woman in global politics. A university professor and expert on Russian history, Rice is known for her cool, calm manner. When Bush appointed her to the job in 2000, some wondered if she was qualified for it. But Janne Nolan, a friend of Rice's from her early days as a Stanford University professor, told *New Yorker* writer Nicholas Lemann that Rice had a solid track record for proving herself. "I've watched it over and over again—the sequential underestimation of Condi," Nolan told Lemann. "It just gets worse and worse. She's always thought of as underqualified and in over her head, and she always kicks everyone's butt."

A job such as Rice's requires nerves of steel, and the French- and Russian-fluent academic, whose friends and family call her "Condi," fits the bill. She explained in an interview with *Essence* writer Isabel Wilkerson, "My parents went to great lengths to make sure I was confident. My mother was also a great believer in being proper." As an African American and a professional, Rice has experienced the occasional racial snub. She recalled one occasion when she asked to see some of the nicer jewelry in a store, and the saleswoman mumbled a rude remark under her breath. As Rice recalled to Wilkerson, she told the woman, "'Let's get one thing clear. If you could afford anything in here, you wouldn't be behind this counter. So I strongly suggest you do your job.'"

The confidence that Rice's parents instilled in her comes out in other ways, too. She favors suits by Italian designer Giorgio Armani, but the trim, fit national security adviser prefers her skirts to hit just above the knee. Her favorite lipstick comes from the Yves Saint Laurent cosmetics counter. When asked about her off-duty hours, Rice told Wilkerson that she watches sports and goes shopping. Wilkerson wondered about the Secret Service security detail that accompanies Rice in public, but Rice responded with a humor rarely on display in public, "They can handle shopping."

the site of a tragic firebombing that killed four little girls who were attending Sunday school. Rice knew two of them.

## Finished high school at fifteen

Rice's family moved to Tuscaloosa, Alabama, around 1965, when she was eleven years old. Her father had taken a job there as a college administrator. They later settled in Denver, Colorado, where she attended an integrated public school for the first time in her life, beginning with the tenth grade. She finished her last year of high school and her first year at the University of Denver at the same time.

For years Rice dreamed of becoming a concert pianist. At the University of Denver she was originally a music major, but eventually gave up on her dream after spending a summer at music camp. "Technically, I can play most anything," she explained to Winfrey about her decision to change majors. "But I'll never play it the way the truly great pianists do." She fell in love with political science and Russian history after she took a class taught by Josef Korbel (1909–1977), a refugee from Czechoslovakia. In the 1990s Korbel's daughter, Madeleine Albright (1937–), became the first female U.S. Secretary of State.

Rice began taking Russian-language and history courses, and became fascinated by Cold War politics. The term refers to the hostilities between the United States and the world's first Communist state, Soviet Russia, in the years following World War II (1939–45). Each "superpower" tried to win allies to its brand of politics, and in the process each side built up a large arsenal of nuclear weapons. After she graduated from the University of Denver in 1974, Rice enrolled at Notre Dame University in Indiana, where she earned a master's degree in government and international studies.

## Drifted for a time

Years later Rice admitted, in the interview with Winfrey, "I am still someone with no long-term plan." To begin her post-college career, she lined up a job as an executive assistant—in other words, a secretary—to a vice president at Honeywell, a large electronics corporation. But a company reorganization ended that career possibility. For a time she gave piano lessons. Then her former professor, Josef Korbel, suggested that she return to school, and she began work on a Ph.D. degree at the University of Denver.

Rice was a promising new talent in her field even before she earned a doctorate in 1981. Her dissertation investigated the relationship between the Czechoslovak Communist Party and its army. Soon she was offered a fellowship at Stanford University. No other woman had ever been offered a fellowship to its Center for International Security and Arms Control. She eagerly accepted, and the following year she was hired by Stanford to teach political science.

Rice became a tenured professor at Stanford in 1987. She was also a rising star in U.S. foreign policy circles. She served as the informal campaign adviser to a Colorado Democrat, Gary Hart (1936–), during his 1984 bid for the White House. She came to know a foreign policy expert, Brent Scowcroft (1925–), and was offered her first official job in government. Scowcroft had been named national security adviser by George H. W. Bush (1924–), who was elected president in 1988. Scowcroft then hired Rice as a staff member on the National Security Council.

## Served in first Bush White House

The National Security Council helps analyze data and plan American foreign policy. It looks at potential global threats from hostile nations, and works to make strategic alliances with friendly ones. Rice eventually became a special assistant to the first President Bush, serving as his expert on Soviet and East European affairs. It was an important time in American foreign policy. The political system of the Soviet Union was crumbling, and by 1991 the Communist governments allied with Soviet Russia had been peacefully ousted throughout the Eastern Bloc (as the communist nations in Eastern Europe were known).

But Rice tired of the toll the White House job took on her personal life, and she resigned in 1991. She went back to teaching at Stanford, and in 1993 became the university's first-ever female provost, which essentially made her second-in-command at the school. She was also the first African American to be selected for the position. "That was the toughest job I ever had," she told Nicholas Lemann in a *New Yorker* profile. She was charged with eliminating a large budget deficit, and the university had also been accused of misusing government grant money intended for military research. There was internal turmoil as well, and some faculty members complained about Rice's no-nonsense manner. "I told people, 'I don't do committees,'" she explained to Lemann.

Rice remained on friendly terms with the Bush family and came to know one of the sons, George W., during visits to the Bush summer home in Kennebunkport, Maine. In 1999 George W. Bush decided to try and win the Republican Party's nomination as its presidential candidate for 2000. He hired Rice to lead his team of foreign policy advisers, and she quit the Stanford job. She began working closely with Bush, who was governor of Texas at the time and had very little other political experience, especially in foreign relations.

Bush won his party's nomination and later was declared the winner of a hotly contested November election. The president-elect immediately named Rice as his national security adviser. Though she was not the first African American ever to hold the post—Bush's new Secretary of State, Colin L. Powell (1937–), had held the job for a year in the late 1980s—she was the first woman ever to serve in the position. The national security adviser helps shape American foreign policy, both on the public front and behind the scenes, in strategy sessions with the president and his team.

## Plotted strategy from underground bunker

Rice's duties also included coming up with ideas to combat threats to American interests at home and overseas. This became an important part of her job on the morning of September 11, 2001. She was in a meeting at the White House when an aide notified her that a plane had struck the World Trade Center. She quickly ended the meeting and notified the President, who was in Florida. After a second plane crashed into the other tower of the New York landmark, she and other key personnel gathered in what is known as the White House "Situation Room." When a third plane crashed into the Pentagon Building, which is the command center for the U.S. Armed Forces, Rice and the others retreated to an underground bunker. The attack was the deadliest ever to occur on American soil.

Rice worked long days in the months afterward to shape U.S. foreign policy. The first order of business involved Afghanistan, which was suspected of harboring the shadowy Islamic fundamentalist group known as Al Qaeda. It was founded by a Saudi exile, Osama bin Laden (1957–), who quickly took responsibility for the 9/11 attacks. Less than a month later, U.S. forces invaded Afghanistan. Rice also worked to create a new policy for dealing with longtime Iraqi leader Saddam Hussein (1937–). The Bush White House believed that Hussein had weapons of mass destruction that could be used against the United States. In March of 2003 the United States invaded Iraq.

The fourth year of the Bush Administration was a difficult one for Rice and other top White House and Pentagon personnel. Though Hussein had been captured and the war in Iraq was officially declared over, U.S. troops stationed in Iraq had become the target of repeated attacks by insurgents. And American military operatives had yet to capture bin Laden. In April of 2004 Rice was called to testify before a

*Condoleezza Rice testifies before the 9/11 Commssion, April 8, 2004.* AP/Wide World Photos. Reproduced by permission.

special panel that had been set up to investigate the 9/11 attacks, namely whether or not the attacks could have been prevented and how the emergency response to such an attack could be improved. There were charges that U.S. intelligence officials may have come across suspicious information but failed to put the pieces together. Rice sat before the official 9/11 Commission, in front of a barrage of television cameras, and held her ground. "There was nothing demonstrating or showing that something was coming in the United States," she asserted, according to the *New York Times*. "If there had been something, we would have acted on it."

## Dreams of top NFL job

Rice lives in a luxury apartment complex in Washington known as Watergate. Her mother died in 1985, and her father died the same month that Bush named her to the national security adviser post. She attends church regularly, and is known to be close to the President and his wife, Laura (1946–). At the Maryland presidential retreat known as Camp David, she has been known to watch hours of televised sports with President Bush. Both are dedicated football fans, and Rice has also been known to spend an entire day on her own watching college and pro football games.

Rice's name has been mentioned as a possible future vice-presidential candidate. Although she has joked that she would love to serve as commissioner of the National Football League, she has also said that she looks forward to returning to teaching once her service to the Bush White House comes to an end. "I miss my kids," she said in the interview with Winfrey. "In a class of 20, there are always two or three for whom the lights go on. When that happens, I think I've done for them what Dr. Korbel did for me."

## For More Information

### Periodicals

Bumiller, Elisabeth. "A Partner in Shaping an Assertive Foreign Policy." *New York Times* (January 7, 2004): p. A1.

"Condi Rice Can't Lose: George W. Bush's Foreign-Policy Adviser Is a Future Superstar. But Can She Save Bush from Himself?" *Time* (September 27, 1999): p. 51.

Lemann, Nicholas. "Without a Doubt. (National-Security Adviser Condoleezza Rice)." *New Yorker* (October 14, 2002).

Lewis, Neil A. "Bush Adviser Backs Use of Race in College Admissions." *New York Times* (Jan 18, 2003): p. A14.

Oppel, Richard A. Jr. "Bush Adviser Gets National Security Post." *New York Times* (December 18, 2000): p. A1.

Sciolino, Elaine. "Compulsion To Achieve—Condoleezza Rice." *New York Times* (December 18, 2000): p. A1.

"Sticking to Their Scripts." *New York Times* (April 9, 2004): p. A1.

Wilkerson, Isabel. "The Most Powerful Woman in the World: As National Security Adviser, Condoleezza Rice Has the Ear of the President. So Who Exactly Is This Daughter of 1960's Birmingham, and What Does She Bring to the Table?" *Essence* (February 2002): p. 114.

Winfrey, Oprah. "Oprah Talks to Condoleezza Rice: Our Calm, Cool, Collected National Security Adviser on Downtime (Piano, Football, Shopping) and Uptime (Faith, Unity, Power)—And Why the Terrorists Have Already Lost. (The O Interview)." *O, The Oprah Magazine* (February 2002): p. 118.

# Andy Roddick

*August 30, 1982* • *Omaha, Nebraska*

## Tennis player

Tennis player Andy Roddick had just turned twenty-one when he won the men's U.S. Open tennis title in September of 2003. The Florida athlete's rugged good looks and down-to-earth personality have helped make him one of the sport's newest celebrities, but it is his athleticism and powerful serve that have propelled him to the highest world rankings in men's tennis. *Sports Illustrated* writer L. Jon Wertheim asserted that Roddick has a new style, far from "the unimaginative, topspin-heavy baseline tennis that, lamentably, has characterized the U.S. juniors over the past 15 years.… Roddick plays Smash Mouth tennis. Armed with a bludgeon for a forehand and with a serve that regularly eclipses 125 [miles per hour], he just, as he puts it, 'whales away out there.'"

## Followed older brother into game

Roddick was born on August 30, 1982, in Omaha, Nebraska, and was the youngest of three boys. His father, Jerry, owned several Jiffy Lube automobile maintenance franchises. The family eventually settled in the Austin, Texas, area, where a very young Roddick took tennis lessons in a group that included two future professional athletes: Chris Mihm (1979–), later of the Boston Celtics, and Drew Brees (1979–), who became a quarterback for the San Diego Chargers. Both, Roddick has joked, were much better players than he was at the time.

Roddick was not the first tennis prodigy in his family. One of his older brothers, John, played on the junior circuit and made it into the top ten in the rankings during his teens. The family even relocated from Austin, Texas, to Florida so that John could train year-round. John was about six years older than Andy, and went on to run a tennis

> "For whatever reason, I play well when it matters most. Toughness has never been a weakness of mine."

academy in San Antonio, Texas, after retiring from competition because of a back injury.

Roddick came from a well-to-do family that could easily afford the expensive lessons and equipment necessary for early training in tennis. He picked up a racket to follow in his brother's footsteps, and was intensely focused from an early age. He begged his mother to let him have a rebound net in the garage. "It had springs. You'd hit the ball and it came back to you," he explained to Neil Harman, a journalist for the London *Times*. "I'd spend hours on it and Mum would ask: 'What did you do today?' I'd say: 'I beat Lendl, Becker, Edberg,'" citing the names of three greats from the men's tennis circuit during the 1980s—Czech player Ivan Lendl (1960–), Boris Becker (1967–) of Germany, and Stefan Edberg (1966–) of Sweden.

For his ninth birthday in 1991, Roddick's parents took him on a trip to Flushing, New York, where they watched the U.S. Open from the stands. "He would wear tennis clothes every day he came here," his mother, Blanche Roddick, recalled to Wertheim. "He got into the

## The Next Sampras

Sportswriters often compare Andy Roddick to Pete Sampras, the American champion who also began beating some of the world's top-ranked players at a very young age. Roddick has often said that Sampras was one of his idols when he was growing up, and his rise has been almost as quick as Sampras's, who won his first U.S. Open tournament at the age of nineteen in 1990. Sampras went on to win a record total of fourteen Grand Slam singles titles over the course of his career.

Watching a young Roddick play, many sportswriters have compared him to Sampras. Both had similar physiques, forceful serves, and a strong forehand that unnerved opponents. Roddick had actually beaten Sampras the first time they ever went up against one another on the court, in March of 2001 at the Ericsson/Lipton ATP tournament in Key Biscayne, Florida.

When Roddick won his first U.S. Open title, in 2003, sportswriters called the event the passing of the torch: Sampras had announced his retirement from professional tennis at the age of 32. He was honored for his achievements at a ceremony that took place on the first day of the Open. Thirteen days later, Roddick won the men's title that Sampras had taken four times before him. "Andy is the future," Sampras told *W* writer Robert Haskell a few months before he retired. "His serve is devastating, and he's got all those intangibles required to be a great player."

players' lounge with no credentials." At the age of fourteen, Roddick attended a tennis camp in Tampa, Florida, but did not like the intensely competitive atmosphere. Nor did he attend one of the well-known Florida tennis academies that train champions during their teen years. Instead he went to a private school near the Roddicks' Boca Raton home, and played on its basketball team.

## Turned pro in 2000

Roddick's talent as a tennis player began to gain attention in late 1999, not long after his seventeenth birthday. He won two juniors titles in Florida, the Orange Bowl and the Eddie Herr International. In January of 2000, he traveled thousands of miles to play in the Australian Open. He was still in the juniors rankings, and surprised many when he became the first American male player since 1959 to win the junior men's title.

Though many colleges tried to recruit Roddick for their tennis programs, he decided to turn professional instead. This also allowed him to sign endorsement contracts with sportswear makers, tennis racket manufacturers, and other companies. In just the second match that Roddick ever played as a pro, he made a surprisingly good showing against one of his heroes, Andre Agassi (1970–), at the Ericsson Open in Key Biscayne, Florida. Agassi beat Roddick, but many sportswriters hailed the teen as the next big star of American tennis.

During the 2001 season Roddick struggled to fulfill that promise. There were several highlights, including the moment when he eliminated another one of his heroes, Michael Chang (1972–), early in the French Open in May. It was a long game that lasted nearly four hours, and halfway through it Roddick began suffering from leg cramps. He seemed to play more fiercely then, commentators noticed. He admitted at the post-match press conference that he had been determined to come out on top. "You don't play three and a half hours to lay down and die when it gets tough," he was quoted as saying by *New York Times* reporter Selena Roberts. "I was telling myself, 'Give it your all until the last ball is over.'"

Roddick failed to advance much further during the 2001 French Open. He was eliminated at Wimbledon and in the quarterfinals of the U.S. Open later that year. Both Opens, along with Wimbledon and the Australian Open, are known as tennis's "Grand Slam" titles. They are the toughest and most prestigious tournaments, watched by millions around the world, and also come with generous cash prizes for a first-place win. In 2002 Roddick once again failed to win any of the Grand Slam titles.

## Changed coaches

In May of 2003, after a disappointing performance in the first round of the French Open, Roddick replaced his longtime French coach, Tarik Benhabiles, with a new pro. Benhabiles had been a strict coach with the teenage Roddick when he needed firm discipline, but Roddick was now twenty years old. He was dating actress-singer Mandy Moore (1984–) at the time, and it was rumored that Benhabiles was trying to limit Roddick's social life in order to keep him focused on his game. But the tactful Roddick claimed that he switched coaches only because he needed more help learning to play on grass courts like Wimbledon. "Our friendship was getting scarred," the athlete told *Sports Illustrated*, "because we weren't getting along tenniswise."

Roddick began working with Brad Gilbert, Agassi's former coach, in June of 2003, and began a winning streak almost immediately. Later that month he made it to the semi-finals on Wimbledon's grass, but was ousted by Roger Federer (1981–) of Switzerland. The next big match-up was in August at the U.S. Open, held in New York at Arthur Ashe Stadium in Flushing Meadows, Queens. Though the tournament was repeatedly delayed by rain-outs, Roddick steadily beat his opponents and then eliminated Juan Carlos Ferrero (1980–) of Spain. At the time, Ferrero was the number one-ranked men's player.

In November of 2003 Roddick played admirably in the Masters Series Cup, and finished the 2003 season as the world's top-ranked men's player. He hosted the NBC series *Saturday Night Live* that same month. In May of 2004, he traveled to Rome, Italy, to play in another Masters Series tournament, where he was awakened by the smell of smoke at his hotel at five A.M. Roddick alerted other guests at the Grand Hotel Parco dei Principi, and took them onto his sixth-floor balcony to

*Andy Roddick, during a semifinal match at the 2004 Siebel Open.* AP/Wide World Photos. Reproduced by permission.

await rescue. He also helped others down from the balcony above his. He was the last one to be rescued by firefighters, and was praised for his heroics during the early morning blaze that killed three guests.

## "The biggest dork"

Later that month, Roddick was dampened by a loss to Olivier Mutis of France at the French Open. At Wimbledon, he broke his own speed record for a serve-153 miles per hour-and made it to the Wimbledon finals for the first time. On July 4, he lost to Federer over four sets. "Roger just played too good today," the *New York Times*'s Christopher Clarey quoted him as saying. "I threw the kitchen sink at him, but he went to the bathroom and got his tub."

Roddick was anticipating defending his U.S. Open title come August of 2004. He realizes that one injury could end his career, which happened with his brother, but his goal is to win a year's worth of Grand Slam titles and help America capture a Davis Cup win. He remains close to his parents, and has used some of the prize money from his winnings to buy a house near both of his older brothers in Austin, Texas. He has legions of fans, and has been the subject of numerous magazine features and photo spreads, but claims to be anything but cool. "You can ask anyone who knows me," he told Roberts. "I'm still the biggest dork that ever lived."

## For More Information

### *Periodicals*

Adkins, Greg. "Splitting: Mandy Moore & Andy Roddick." *People* (March 29, 2004): p. 26.

Battista, Judy. "One Shot Is What Roddick Needed." *New York Times* (April 2, 2004): p. D6.

Bierley, Stephen. "Wimbledon 2003: The 117th Championships: Roddick Brings New Power to His Elbow and His Aces: The Young American Has Acquired the Look of a Champion." *Guardian* (London, England) (June 23, 2003): p. 1.

Bricker, Charles. "Boca Raton's Roddick Is the Teenager of the Hour." Knight Ridder/Tribune News Service (June 3, 2000): p. K5516.

Clarey, Christopher. "Federer's 2nd Title Just as Sweet." *New York Times* (July 5, 2004): p. D1.

Clarey, Christopher. "Henin-Hardenne and Roddick Ousted." *New York Times* (May 27, 2004): p. D1.

Dicker, Ron. "Rah-Rah Roddick Happy to Be Part of New Generation in the Davis Cup." *New York Times* (February 9, 2004): p. D7.

Harman, Neil. "Roddick Takes His Place Among the Great Names." *Times* (London, England) (September 9, 2003): p. 35.

Haskell, Robert. "Hot Roddick: With a Potent Game, Heartthrob Looks and a Personality That Fills Stadiums, Andy Roddick May Be the Savior of Men's Tennis." *W* (April 2003): p. 270.

John, Elton. "Andy Roddick: The Two Stadium-Packin' Headliners—One a Legendary Tunesmith, the Other, Tennis's Next Legend in the Making—Talk Work and Play. (Elton John interviews tennis player)." *Interview* (July 2003): p. 56.

Roberts, Selena. "After Opponent's Rant, Roddick Shows Class." *New York Times* (August 31, 2003): p. SP4.

Roberts, Selena. "No. 1 Is a Role Roddick Is Playing for Keeps." *New York Times* (November 14, 2003): p. D3.

Roberts, Selena. "Roddick Conquers Cramps, and Childhood Hero." *New York Times* (May 31, 2001): p. D5.

"Roddick's Fire Rescue." *People* (May 17, 2004): p. 18.

Vecsey, George. "A Brash Young American Comes of Age, and Cries." *New York Times* (September 8, 2003): p. D11.

Wertheim, L. Jon. "Andy Roddick Is Just Like You: Well, Except for Being the U.S. Open Champion and Being Ranked No. 1 in the World and Dating Mandy Moore. Other Than That, He's Everyman." *Sports Illustrated* (November 10, 2003): p. 72.

Wertheim, L. Jon. "Long Live The King: Andy Roddick, the Crown Prince of the American Game, Finally Assumed the Throne with a Commanding Victory in the U.S. Open Final." *Sports Illustrated* (Sept 15, 2003): p. 56.

Wertheim, L. Jon. "Rare Specimen Found in Florida: Andy Roddick Is the First American Boy to Win the Australian Junior since 1959." *Sports Illustrated* (Feb 21, 2000): p. R6 .

### Web Sites

*Andy Roddick Official Web site.* http://www.andyroddick.com/ (accessed on June 9, 2004).

*Volume numbers are in* italic; ***boldface*** *indicates main entries and their page numbers; (ill.) following a page number indicates an illustration on the page.*

# J

# ◉

# P

**q**